How to Master Essential Life skills

Skillsets for Success, Volume 1

DR. K. V. SAHASRANAM

Published by Sahasranam Kalpathy, 2023.

HOW TO MASTER ESSENTIAL LIFE SKILLS

First edition. November 27, 2023.

Copyright © 2023 DR. K. V. SAHASRANAM.

ISBN: 979-8215238639

Written by DR. K. V. SAHASRANAM.

How to Master Essential Life skills

Management Insights for Healthcare Professionals
Drawn from a Medical Director's Memoirs

Skillsets for Success -Book 1

Dr. K. V. Sahasranam MD. DM. FACC.

Dedication
To my Late Parents –
My unwavering pillars of strength,
whose boundless love and unwavering support
have sculpted the foundation of my journey.
Through every triumph and trial, their
guidance has been my compass.
This book stands as a testament to the
immeasurable impact of their nurturing
hands on my life.

PREFACE

In the autumn of 2013, while I was deeply immersed in my consultation, I was urgently summoned to the august chambers of the Chairman and Managing Director of the hospital, Dr Alexander. Upon my arrival, I was greeted by the CEO of the hospital, Dr Soman Jacob, who was already seated in attendance. After the customary pleasantries, I was informed of the purpose of this momentous conclave.

"The management has decided to promote you to the exalted position of Chief of Medical Services at this hospital," the chairman decreed. "You shall assume charge on the first day of the coming month."

I was struck dumb with astonishment. My meager managerial experience left me woefully unprepared to oversee the two hundred and fifty-odd physicians under my purview, let alone the postgraduate trainees who would be entrusted to my care.

"But, Sir, I have no training in people management," I stammered, "And I am uncertain whether I am capable of fulfilling the duties of the CMS post."

"Do not fret," Dr Jacob reassured me with a calming smile. "You will learn as you go along, and we will be there to guide you."

Thus began my perilous journey as the Chief of Medical Services at the Baby Memorial Hospital, a 600-bed multidisciplinary healthcare facility in the metropolis of Kozhikode, nestled within the diminutive bitter gourd-shaped state of Kerala in South India.

Having served at the hospital for the past seventeen years as a senior Cardiologist, this unexpected elevation came as a heavy burden, leaving me overwhelmed and apprehensive about my ability to discharge the administrative responsibilities entrusted to me.

The munificent CEO, Dr. Soman Jacob, freely imparted his tutelage in the rudiments of administration and inculcated in me the requisite acumen to orchestrate the sizable contingent of physicians.

Over the span of a few months, he mentored me, and I acquired the wherewithal to efficaciously execute the assignments entrusted to me.

When Dr. Jacob relinquished his post, Ms. Gracy Mathai, the succeeding CEO, facilitated my ascendance as CMS through her sagacious guidance. She was instrumental in navigating me through the labyrinthine maze of management skills and administrative duties. Mr. Saji Mathew, the COO, was a congenial confidant and mentor, imparting his boundless erudition in management principles and acumen, much of which accrued to me during my association with him.

Post-retirement, I felt compelled to chronicle my experiences and impart my skills to hospital staff and the general public through journaling. This humble endeavor is a testament to my desire to share my knowledge and expertise.

In this tome, I have elucidated on some of the essential skills that hospital employees should possess. This treatise is not exclusively for doctors and nurses, but also for all non-medical hospital staff. The general reader, the student, the teacher and even the humble self-effacing housewife can derive benefit from this work of mine.

Some of the skills delineated in this book, such as Time Management and Communication Skills, are the sine qua non for achieving success in life. Others, such as Interpersonal Relationships, are an integral facet of daily human interaction. Conflicts are ubiquitous in everyday life, ranging from minor altercations to major discords that can engender professional tribulations. In the healthcare setting, conflicts between patients and healthcare providers are not uncommon, and management is often called upon to arbitrate.

In a hospital care setting, communication between physicians, nurses, patients, and their families is paramount, as any lacunae in communication can precipitate complaints and litigation. Healthcare providers must exercise extreme circumspection to be candid and transparent in their communication. Clinical Handover is another crucial aspect of healthcare that ensures patient safety.

Above all, stress is a ubiquitous emotion that everyone experiences to varying degrees. No profession is exempt from the rigors of stress. Each individual's response to this ubiquitous emotion is unique. Effective Stress Management is essential in a hospital setting. Stress management is therefore paramount for all individuals involved in healthcare.

I have recounted some anecdotal instances that I had to navigate with diplomacy and tact during my tenure. Some of the anecdotes are from my experiences prior to working in the private multispecialty hospital. My journaling experience has assisted me in chronicling these experiences. To preserve anonymity, I have altered the names of the individuals involved and their designations.

I aspire that this humble endeavor will prove to be a valuable resource for all hospital staff and other healthcare professionals.

I appeal to the readers, after critically appraising this book, to bestow upon me a candid evaluation of their opinion. Such frank reviews will be a boon, spurring me to author more works in this series, aptly titled "**Skillsets for Success.**"

With these words, I submit my book before my readers.

Dr. K. V. Sahasranam.

INTRODUCTION

Skill is the ability to do something well. It is the competence in performance. Technical skills are essential for success in any career, such as the clinical skills of a doctor, the flying skills of a pilot, the coding skills of an IT professional or the design skills of an engineer. These skills are acquired through academic coursework and subsequent training.

However, 'People Management Skills', also known as 'Soft Skills', are equally important for success in any walk of life. These skills are essential for interacting with and managing people effectively, whether you are a manager, employee, student, self-employed professional, or housewife.

Communication and *Time Management* are two of the most important soft skills that anyone who aspires to success in any walk of life should develop. Developing the skills needed to interact with others and manage oneself is essential for achieving one's goals in any career.

This book is written for employees and middle-level managers in any organization, regardless of their industry. It is important to note that skills are not innate; they are developed through constant training and practice. Those who do not invest time in developing their skills will be left behind in their careers with diminished prospects for advancement.

The book is written in the context of a healthcare organization, but the skills it describes are equally relevant to non-medical employees, doctors, and nurses. These skills are also applicable to any person working in any organization, regardless of industry.

Students, academics, teachers, and housewives alike can benefit from the skills described in this book. *Interpersonal Skills*, *Communication*, and *Time Management* are essential for everyone who wants to carve out a successful career.

Stress Management is just as important for the housewife who manages her school-going children as it is for the CEO of a multinational corporation. _Work-life balance_ is a crucial skill for all executives, as it is at the core of a fulfilling life. The saying "_All work and no play makes Jack a dull boy_" confirms that work-life balance is the foundation of stress management.

Conflicts are an inevitable part of life, no matter how minor. _Conflict Management_ is essential for everyone, from executive leadership and teachers to self-employed skilled workers and white-collar employees. This book covers the important principles of conflict management in considerable detail.

Communication skills are equally or more important in a healthcare setting, where doctors and nurses, who are the primary healthcare providers, must be exceptionally trained in this area. _Doctor-patient communication_ is discussed in detail in this book. One of the most challenging aspects of being a physician is conveying Bad News to patients or their family members. This topic is covered in the chapter on _Breaking Bad News_, which provides a practical and structured approach to delivering difficult news.

Transferring patients from one healthcare provider to another or to another facility requires transferring accountability and responsibility while ensuring adequate continuity of care. This is covered in the chapter on _Clinical Handover_, which discusses methods of handing over patients in detail, including their condition and medications.

This book is intended to be a guide for healthcare providers and other employees in the healthcare sector. It is not a comprehensive book on management, but it is helpful for employees, middle-level managers, and supervisors who do not have training in skill management. Dealing with patients and their families is an important part of the duties of employees in the healthcare sector, from the receptionist at the front desk to the doctors, nurses, technicians, and other workers.

Healthcare professionals, such as medical students, junior doctors, residents, nursing students, and nurses, have direct contact with patients and their families. They should have the skills to deal with a wide range of patients from different cultures, ethnic groups, and religions, with varying educational backgrounds and attitudes. This requires patience and resilience. All healthcare employees should develop the emotional intelligence to manage their own emotions and attitudes. This book provides a few tips and guides to help readers hone their people management skills.

1. Mastering the Clock – TIME MANAGEMENT

One of the important skills that one needs to master in having a successful career is time management. Time is a precious non-renewable resource that cannot be stored for future use. Once lost, it is lost forever. Thus, managing, organizing, and distributing time for various tasks is a skill that can be developed by deliberately training oneself. Time management becomes important whether you are a professional, student or a housewife. In every walk of life, managing one's time becomes important in having a stress-free life. When you use time wisely, you work smarter and better. Twenty-four hours is the time we get daily whatever be your calling in life and wise is the man who learns to judiciously apportion these 24 hours to tasks to achieve success and happiness in his life. You make 'time' work for you when you manage it properly.

Definition: Time Management has been variously defined as "_the process of planning and exercising control over the amount of time spent on specific activities to increase effectiveness, efficiency and productivity_". Simply put, it means using the time available in a useful and effective way.

Time Audit.

Time management assumes importance in our day to day activities in living a stress-free life. It helps us understand how we spend our time and identify areas where our time is wasted. It also helps us prioritize our tasks and get our tasks completed on time. It helps us in our decision making and also helps us balance our life and work. It helps us in our decision making too.

Before delving into time management, conducting a Time Audit is crucial. A Time Audit will appropriately tell us the amount of time we apportion to each of our tasks. For a week or two, one should keep track of the time spent for each of the daily tasks and make a note of this. By the end of this audit we can be sure how much time we spend for each of our activities. This often is an eye-opener for us indicating the amount of time of time we spend for each of our activities and also the amount of time that we waste daily on activities like gossiping, social media, lazing around or aimless TV watching.

Proper time management is a combination of *Processes*, *Tools*, *Techniques* and *Methods* and when properly planned and applied to our day to day tasks, it can prove a blessing.

Time Wasters : Time wasters are tasks that drain our valuable time without providing any effective returns. In a study in the US, it was found that an average worker 'wasted' 2.09 hours out of the 8 hour working day. Time wasters come in various forms. We can categorize them into two main types for better understanding.

Internal Time Wasters :

These result from the inadequacy or idiosyncrasy of the individual. Some individuals exhibit disorganization, cluttered desks, lack of task planning, or attend unprepared meetings, squandering both their time and that of others.

Unnecessary procrastination of tasks due to lack of self-confidence, fear of making a wrong decision or fear of failure can waste a person's time. *'Imposter Syndrome'* is another cause for wasted time where the individual doubts his own skills and accomplishments and hence is at a loss in carrying out a task successfully due to uncertainty and self-doubt.

Excessive socialization during office hours, spending significant time gossiping and interacting with colleagues before starting work, negatively impacts work quality and focus.

Some employees are not skillful in communicating and hence are not able to get their point across. They do not listen properly and are not able to communicate effectively with their colleagues and managers. This often results in time lost from work as duplication of work often occurs due to the poor quality of work.

Personal inefficiency, often stemming from a lack of skills or talent, can hinder quick decision-making and effective task execution.

External Time Wasters:

These are circumstances which are beyond the control of the individual. They are often encountered in office settings. Poorly planned, unnecessary, or excessively long meetings, where some participants may not need to attend, are time-wasting factors.

Work interruptions, a common challenge beyond an employee or manager's control, include unexpected visitors, lengthy phone calls, and outdated technology, all contributing to wasted time.

In settings like hospitals, unforeseen emergencies, though not precisely time wasters, can disrupt planned duties for doctors and nurses, leading to the procrastination of other critical tasks and disrupting time management.

It is crucial to remember the 80/20 principle: **80% of tasks can be accomplished in 20% of your time, while the remaining 20% of tasks may consume 80% of your time.**

Skills Needed In Time Management.

Proper time management necessitates the development of various skills by both employees and managers within an organization. These skills are crucial for optimizing time usage and minimizing wastage. Key skills include planning and prioritizing activities, avoiding procrastination, maintaining a To-Do List, setting clear goals, proper scheduling, refraining from multitasking, delegating tasks, and reviewing progress. In this discussion, we will describe the skills essential for effective time management in an office setting.

Prioritization and Planning.

Achieving optimal time management is accomplished by those who diligently plan and prioritize their daily, weekly, and monthly tasks.

Scheduling

Creating a schedule for the day and sticking to it often gives us enough time to accomplish most of our tasks. *One who fails to plan, plans to fail*. A schedule should encompass work-related, personal, and recreational activities, as well as time for reading and replying to emails, making phone calls, preparing memos, and reading the newspaper. Identifying one's most efficient time of day for focused and intensive mental activity is crucial.

Most people find the first few hours of the morning the most important time when they are able to focus and concentrate on tasks that require thinking and intense mental activity. The entire day can be structured to maximize efficiency, incorporating necessary breaks such as coffee breaks and lunch breaks.

Tools may be used in scheduling one's daily tasks. Many apps and tools are available. Google Calendar, Calendly, and other online tools are available for task scheduling. The simple method of putting down your daily schedule on a planner, pocket diary, notebook, index card or any other method of one's choice may be used. When a tool is used, every task should be recorded in one place and not in multiple sites. If using electronic apps a tool which synchronizes with your mobile device, laptop and computer may be ideal as this will make the schedule accessible on the move. The tasks should be listed and prioritized using color coding for ease of recognition.

When scheduling tasks, including a buffer time between them is vital. When working continuously, short breaks of five minutes may be taken using the *Pomodoro technique* which is working for 25 minutes continuously and taking a break of 5 minutes at the end. This is continued for two or three cycles when a break of 15 minutes is taken. The *Pomodoro App* can be downloaded onto one's mobile phone or other device. The five-minute break may be used for a quick cup of coffee, a short walk or to send a message or return a telephone call. This breaks the monotony of working continuously on a task. This technique aids focus and productivity.

To-Do-List

Creating a daily list of tasks, whether digitally or on paper, is a fundamental skill. Taking five minutes in the morning to list tasks, including work, personal, and other activities, has several advantages. There are many advantages of having a To-do-List for the day. It avoids having to remember all tasks that need to be done. It gives a larger picture of what is scheduled for the day at a glance, saves time and avoid forgetting any task which you are likely to overlook. It helps to keep you focused on your priorities and prevents you from side tracking into other activities. It gives you a feeling of self-control and you have a list of things that you have completed.

I always initiate my day with a 'To-Do List.' Carrying a compact booklet in my pocket wherever I go, I promptly record any thoughts or requests that arise throughout the day. Each evening, I review the list, marking off completed tasks. Unfinished items are transferred to the next day's list. I cultivated this practice during my Cardiology residency at the esteemed Post Graduate Institute in Chandigarh, northern India. The Chief of Cardiology, a prominent figure, consistently had a To-Do List in his pocket, noting down any relevant points. Inspired by him, I adopted this habit, which has served me well over the years.

- Tasks on the To-Do List can be categorized by priority – High, Medium, and Low E.g., a meeting with the CEO, a Strategic meeting of the executives or an interview for selecting a new candidate could be a high priority task.
- Preparing for the next training session, giving feedback to an employee could be classed as medium priority.
- Checking the WhatsApp messages or social media, booking your next car maintenance service and planning for your next vacation could be low priority for the day.
- They can also be color-coded or highlighted for easy identification of importance. As tasks are completed, they can be scored off the list.
- At the end of the day, you can take stock and find how successful you have been in managing your time. Any unfinished tasks that could not be accomplished during the day should be included in a to-do-list prepared for the next day.

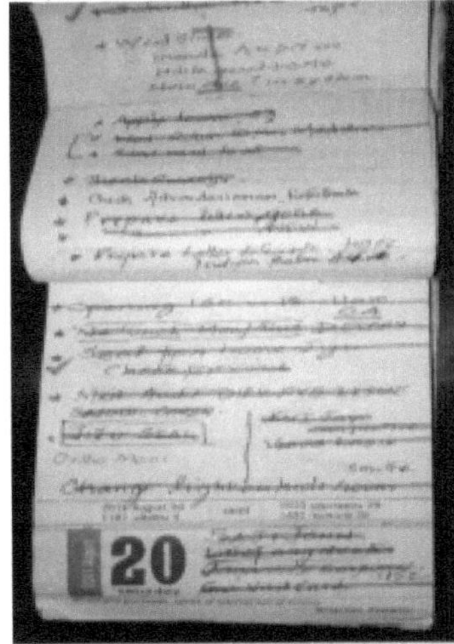

To-Do-List

- 　　　　　　　　　　　　　Always carry a digital organizer or pocket diary to note tasks while in the office or on the go. This ensures tasks are included in the overall time management plan.

Eisenhower Matrix.

The Eisenhower Matrix is a task management tool designed to aid in organizing tasks based on their urgency and importance. Named after Dwight D. Eisenhower, the 34th president of the United States and former general in the U.S. Army, this approach stems from his experiences making critical decisions during his military service. In essence, it categorizes tasks into four quadrants, each signifying a different level of urgency and importance.

Eisenhower's task divisions are as follows:

1. <u>Do it First</u>: Involves tasks of high importance and urgency, to be completed on the same day.
2. <u>Schedule:</u> Encompasses tasks that are important but not immediately urgent, requiring scheduling.
3. <u>Delegate</u>: Pertains to tasks that are urgent but less important; these can be delegated to others.
4. <u>Don't Do</u>: Involves tasks that are neither urgent nor important, suggesting they should be avoided.

The Eisenhower matrix serves as a valuable tool for prioritizing tasks, helping individuals determine which ones to delegate or postpone for later.

1. Urgent + Imp

> Code Blue in hospital
> Emergency Surgery
> Meet Deadline
> Meeting with Chairman
> Draw cash from Bank

2.Not-Urg+ Imp

> Relationship building
> Search for new opportunities
> Elective Surgery
> Exercise for Health
> Annual Medical check

3. Urgent + Not Imp

> Interruptions
> Some mails – Reports
> Some meetings
> Solving others' problem
> Buying groceries.

4. Not Urg+Not Imp

> Trivia
> Some emails/ letters
> WhatsApp messages
> Facebook
> Watching TV
> Read Magazines.

The Eisenhower matrix serves as a valuable tool for prioritizing tasks, helping individuals determine which ones to delegate or postpone for later.

Procrastination.

Delaying or postponing a task which has to be completed is called Procrastination. It is a sign of poor time management and can lead to low productivity, missed deadlines, and increases one's chances of failure. Often this is due to being distracted from work by other timewasters, waiting for the last moment before deciding to complete a task, tendency to put off an unpleasant task and poor planning.

To combat procrastination, consider these strategies:

- Be well organized with your time. Plan ahead as to what tasks have to be completed.
- Keep all materials and work tools needed before beginning your work. Prepare in advance. This would prevent you from postponing the work for lack of resources or tools.
- When you have to complete a 'big' task, always do the small tasks accompanying it first. Ease into larger tasks gradually.

This way, completing the task becomes easy.

- Find out why you tend to procrastinate certain tasks. The answer itself may be an eye opener for the solution. If the task is too overwhelming, break it up into small manageable segments which can be tackled and completed in short periods of time.
- Select a time and place where you want to do your tasks if you are a student or if you are working from home. Avoid distractions like the mobile devices and social media. Identify procrastination triggers and take special pains to avoid them. Some of the procrastination triggers are anxiety and fear, aversion towards the task, low self-esteem, feeling overwhelmed, lack of intrinsic reward for you and task being

ambiguous.

- Always prioritize important tasks and allot a specific time period to complete it.
- Don't aim at perfection in doing a task. Completing a task is better than not doing it at all. Trying to be perfect and feeling anxious about it is a sure way to get it postponed. Complete the task and edit it later at a convenient time.
- Address challenging tasks early in the day when your mind is fresh. This will deter you from postponing it.
- If it is a tough task that you tend to procrastinate, promise yourself a reward after completing it successfully. The reward could be half an hour of TV time late in the evening, a treat at your favorite restaurant, a piece of cake from the fridge or a ticket to a movie of your choice. Incentivizing yourself can thus prevent you from postponing challenging and unpleasant tasks.
- Try the "5-minute" rule. Commit to working on a task for a short period of only 5 minutes. This short period will make the task more manageable. Once you have begun the task and completed 5 minutes, then you will be able to complete the task effectively without procrastinating it.

Upon finishing and publishing a book, I experience a profound sense of self-satisfaction and gratification. To motivate myself, I traditionally organize a family dinner at a chosen restaurant and indulge in a compelling movie on platforms like Netflix or Hulu. This ritual provides the impetus I need to embark on my next literary endeavor after a week.

Multitasking.

The performance of more than one task at a time is called Multitasking. Even though it appears to be an attractive concept to be able to do more than one task at a time, it is not ideal to multitask as it can seriously affect productivity and efficiency. Focusing on one task at a time, hence is much more effective and productive. Research has shown that multitaskers are more distractable than those who do not. In reality, multitasking slows down a person's ability to perform a task. Neither task gets done in time. Even though benefits of multitasking in the form of saving time and money are mentioned, it is not a viable option to focused, concentrated task completion.

Multitasking may be dangerous in certain situations as in speaking on the mobile phone or texting while driving. This can cause serious accidents. Multitaskers are also prone to more mistakes. Workplace efficiency requires vigilant avoidance of multitasking.

Some of the ways we can avoid multitasking are:

- Tasks requiring focus and concentration should not be done together. E.g. driving and texting ; drafting an email while on the phone.
- Use the "20-minute Rule". Instead of multitasking, spend 20 minutes doing one task and switch to the other task with focus.
- Resist the tendency to multitask like checking email or messages while you are working and allocate dedicated slots for these activities.
- Practicing mindfulness and being closely aware of what you are doing helps to avoid multitasking. It helps you enhance focus on singular tasks.
- Following a time schedule for your work and proper time management can avoid multitasking and make it redundant.

A well-focused completion of a task is better compared to two tasks sloppily done.

Tips for Improving Time Management Skills.

There are a few other tips which when practiced in the workplace or in one's daily life, can help you manage your time and tasks properly and without hassle. Some of these are:

- **Time Blocking :** This is a technique where your day is divided into small manageable blocks of time allotted to specific tasks. During each such blocks of time, only one task is done with focus and concentration. The tasks that are difficult and needing mental focus can be planned for the early morning shift when our mental capacities are at peak levels. Other activities not requiring strenuous mental activity can be planned for the noon and evening hours.

- **Batching your time :** This is where you try to plan to do similar activities together to streamline workflow. Grouping tasks which are similar makes doing them easier without spending too much time and effort. E.g., planning a meeting, creating a list of invitees, agenda for the meeting all can be batched together to be done at a particular time.

- **Delegating :** This is mainly to save time for the manager. Many tasks which need not be directly done by a manager can be delegated to suitable employees in the organization. While delegating, specific tasks can be allotted to individuals who have the resources to do them. E.g. A person with a technical IT background can be tasked with the creation of electronic data for the meeting, another person can be tasked with the editing and formatting of a report prepared by the manager. A third person can be given the task of preparing slides for the presentation. While delegating, care should be taken to allot the task to the appropriate candidate who will be able to complete the task successfully in the time allotted. He should be given a specific deadline to complete the task and provided any assistance or resources needed for successful completion of the task.

- **Outsourcing** : Outsourcing is engaging an outside agency or external expertise for completing a task. This helps in saving time for the manager and the employees. E.g. Creating and maintaining a website for the organization is a task that can be outsourced. Auditing of accounts is another task that can be outsourced.

- **Being Organized** : This is an important skill needed in Time Management. Disorganized persons manage time very poorly. One's workplace should be neat and tidy. Unnecessary clutter should be avoided on the table. Things not needed should be either given away or thrown away. Super achievers are said to be super organized. The laptop or desktop computer should also be properly organized with files sorted and saved in proper accessible folders. The desktop of the computer should be uncluttered. Utilizing color coding and flagging are also methods to keep information organized efficiently.

- **Learn to say "No"** : Many of us have a tendency to help other colleagues in the organization. Granted that it is a good idea to help others, it should not be at the expense of one's own time and work. If the task can be done by another person instead of you, delegate it.

If you find that your To-Do-List for the day is long, then politely decline requests for help from others. Offer to help a colleague or do a task for him only if you have the time to do it. Decline requests if necessary. Keep your priorities foremost.

- **Don't waste time waiting** : You may at times find that you have to wait to meet your boss in his cabin. You can use this time fruitfully to read an article that you have been wanting to read or listen to an important podcast which will add value to your work. Value your time. Even short periods of time can be put to productive use.

- **Creative Downtime :** A short period of time daily can be spent to create ideas. A quiet time during a busy schedule of work can be allotted for thinking and contemplating on new ideas for work. This time can be used to brainstorm oneself for newer ideas and concepts. An idea for a new book, a new concept for marketing, a design for the book cover, a new topic for employee training, can all be thought out during this creative downtime. Spare time helps improve your mood, boost your performance, and increase the ability to concentrate and focus on other tasks. During this time the brain reorganizes its memories and information and consolidates them. Sleep is the main downtime for the brain daily. But short breaks during an active workday also provide enough downtime to boost performance and productivity.

- **Minimize Distractions :** One must be able to identify the distractions that may disturb one's focus and productivity in office and try to eliminate them. Many of the distractions have been discussed under 'Time Wasters'. These need to be addressed properly. Notifications in your computer and mobile devices may be turned off if needed to work uninterruptedly. Clutter in the workplace itself can pose a distraction to many. Keep your desk clean. Apps may help you block out distractions. *Forest*, *StayFocused* and *Freedom* are apps that can help you stay focused on your job.

- **Visitors :** Drop in visitors may take up your time. They can be from the office or from outside and may talk about unimportant matters because they have time to kill. Don't give in to them. Find out a method to tackle them. Tell them that you are busy and will contact them later. Or stand up as if you are leaving for a meeting and they will get up and leave.

> While employed at a bustling hospital, I allocated my afternoons for administrative tasks, seizing the quiet period when patients weren't slated for appointments. Nevertheless, there were acquaintances, both from my social and professional circles, who had a habit of dropping by my office unannounced, citing a desire to "catch up."
>
> This tended to disrupt my concentration and workflow. To counteract this, I devised a strategy. I instructed my office assistant to intervene precisely five minutes after the unanticipated visitor, or 'distractor,' arrived. She would then announce that I was urgently needed in the Echocardiographic laboratory. In response, I would promptly stand up, creating the impression that I was about to leave the room. This polite but harmless charade facilitated the 'distractor's' departure without causing any discomfort or disruption to my work.

Another way to get rid of a distractor is to sum up the discussion and shake hands with the person. It gives the impression that the meeting is over. The best way is to have a fixed time for such visitors

- **Telephone Conversations:** Be brief and to the point while speaking on the phone. Don't socialize on the phone or on the computer. Find out who is calling before answering your phone. Have a "No Interruption" time if possible, during the day when you leave word not to be interrupted.

> I used to arrange meetings in the afternoon from 3 to 4 pm, specifically reserved for appointments with medical and pharmaceutical personnel or other visitors. I also kept this time slot open for unscheduled visitors, allowing flexibility. This practice afforded me uninterrupted work periods at other times without offending anyone.

- **End of Day 'Housekeeping' :** At the end of the day when most of the tasks are accomplished and you are ready to call it a day, sit down for 5 – 10 minutes to summarize and review your day's work. Check your to-do-list and see if all your tasks have been completed. Almost always, there may be incomplete tasks due to various reasons beyond your control. Make the next day's To-Do-List and write these tasks down. There may be files to save, sort and organize. Finish these sundry pieces or work at the end of the day. If you have any new tasks lined up for the next day, include them in the new list. See that your table and desktop are clean before you leave your office for the day. This end of day review helps you reflect upon the tasks for the day and recognize any mistakes made in the use of time.

Interestingly, the time we spend per day on important and crucial tasks takes up 20% of our time whereas 80% of the time is spent on tasks which are of little value and less important. It has been noted that an average person in an office is interrupted about 7 – 8 times per hour. It has been shown that 10- 12 minutes used in the morning for planning the day will save about 2 hours of wasted time and effort during the course of the day.

Time management thus becomes one of the most crucial and vital skills that everyone has to develop, whether they are working in an office, a hospital as a doctor, nurse, or an office staff or if one is a homemaker. Proper time management goes a long way in achieving our goals effectively and efficiently. One learns to do more in less time and work without stressing oneself. It also boosts our self-confidence and conserves and increases our energy levels.

"The bad news is time flies. The good news is you're the pilot"
– Michael Altshuler

2. Unlocking the Power of Words – COMMUNICATION

"Excellent communication doesn't just happen naturally. It is a product of process, skill, climate, relationship, and hard work"
– Pat McMillan, author, CEO

Communication skills are the foundation of good management. It is the most sought after skill in management. Whatever technical and talents a person has, without communication skills, he becomes a failure in management. It is known that when Jeff Bezos was setting up Amazon he had insisted on writing skills and ordered *"narratively structured memos"* to be used. Indira Nooyi, CEO of Pepsico says, *"You cannot over invest in communication skills – written or oral skills"*. Improper and ineffective communication skills in the workplace may sometimes turn to be costly errors for the organization. A good leader should always be a good communicator skilled in its intricacies and nuances. Thinking with clarity and expressing his thoughts in an easily comprehensible way is the skill which every leader should possess.

Communication does not mean mere 'speaking'. It is an efficient and effective exchange of ideas and information. It is about interpersonal relationships and creating connections between individuals and teams. In every aspect of management like Conflict Resolution, Negotiation, Giving feedback, Motivating workers, Making Presentations and many more, communication takes the forefront amongst all needed skills. Proper communication is absolutely essential to prevent misunderstandings in the workplace among individuals, teams, and the management.

In the healthcare sector, communication assumes paramount importance as the safety of the customer i.e. the patient, is of utmost significance to the healthcare provider and any fault or drawback in communication can adversely affect the outcome of the patient management process with disastrous results both for the patient and the provider.

Definition: _Communication is the process of exchanging ideas, messages, information, and feelings between two or more persons._ When a person communicates with another person, it is not mere words which are transmitted, but also feelings of the individual are conveyed during the process of communication. This often is missed by the casual listener.

Process of Communication.

Communication is a process that involves many steps. They are as follows:

Sender : It is the person who initiates the communication process.

Encoding: The sender encodes the message in his mind and decides how to communicate his idea. It can be verbal, written or even by gesturing.

Message: It is the content or the information that is to be communicated.

Channel: It is the method used to communicate like speech, written message, email, formal letter etc.

Receiver: It is the person who receives the message.

Decoding: It is the recognition and understanding of the message by the person who receives the message.

Feedback: It is the acknowledgement given by the person who receives the message indicating that the message has been received and understood. It can be in the form of a verbal or written response or a simple nod of the head to acknowledge the message.

During speaking to another person during communication, the words spoken are important and form 7% of the process. The majority of the process of communication is the body language (55%) and the voice of the speaker (38%) which carries more influence.

Feedback

Sender
Encoding
Decoding
Process
Of
Communication
Message
Receiver
Channel

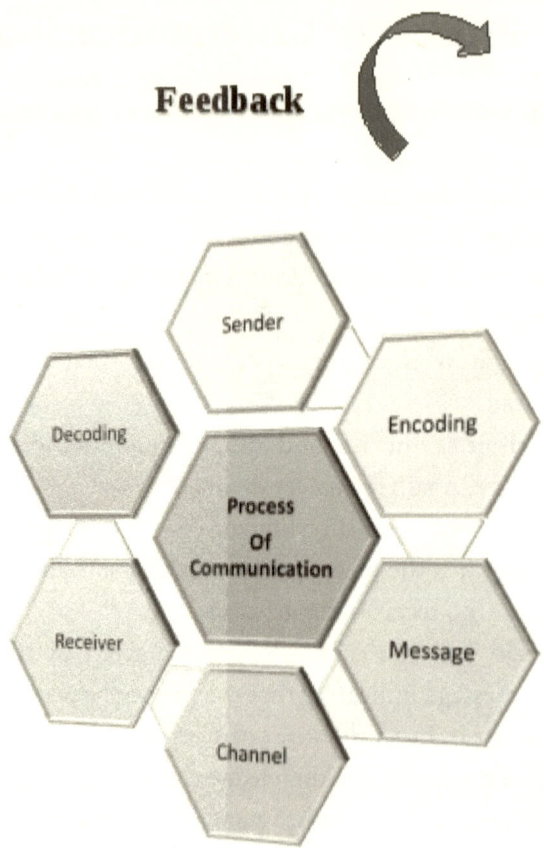

Types Of Communication

For purposes of clarity, communication can be divided into the following types.

Verbal communication

In verbal communication the speaker conveys his message using words which the receiver can understand by listening or seeing. The message can be conveyed directly through speech or through video, telephone, radio, television etc.

Non-verbal communication where the speaker conveys his emotions and feeling during the communication using his body language, gestures, tone of voice, and facial expression. It is communication without words.

Visual communication where visuals like posters or pictures are used to convey a message. There may not be a direct interaction between the sender and the receiver.

Written communication where the message is conveyed through the written medium like email, formal letter, reports, memos etc.

Non-Verbal Communication.

The importance of non-verbal communication lies in the fact that while speaking, 35% of the message is conveyed using the words whereas 65% of the message is conveyed through non-verbal means.

Non-verbal communication encompasses gestures, facial expressions, and eye contact, among other elements. These convey the emotions and attitudes of the communicator, often complementing or emphasizing spoken words. Non-verbal cues persist throughout a conversation, with their interpretation influenced by cultural variations. At times, these cues are crucial for understanding an individual's attitude and feelings.

To enhance non-verbal communication skills, consider the following approaches:

- Maintain eye contact when speaking to someone, rotating attention when addressing multiple individuals. However, avoid prolonged eye contact, limiting it to three to five seconds per person to prevent discomfort.

- Use a tone of voice consistent with the conveyed message, ensuring clarity and proper pronunciation. Adjust the volume appropriately, avoiding speaking too loudly to a small audience.

- Be sure that your facial expressions align with the message you are conveying. Smile when appropriate.

- Nod your head when the other person speaks, to give him the impression that you are actively involved in the conversation.

- Monitor body language, avoiding a rigid posture and maintaining an upright stance. Refrain from crossing your arms, as it may signal disinterest. Keep gestures minimal and context-appropriate, avoiding frowning or furrowing your brow.

- 'Mirroring' is a method where you match the body language, tone and energy level of the other person while communicating one-to-one with him. This fosters likability and trustworthiness.

- In non-verbal communication, paralanguage refers to how people express themselves, considering intonation, pitch, and volume. For instance, the emphasis on specific words in a sentence alters its meaning. As an example, consider the sentence below. The bold letters indicate the words which are emphasized when spoken. The meaning of the sentence changes when the emphasis on the words change. Read the sentence aloud emphasizing each of the words highlighted by turns. You will notice that the meaning of the sentence changes with the emphasis.

I never said that - (I didn't say that; someone else did)

I **never** said that - (I didn't say that at all. I am innocent.)

I never **said** that - (I did not say it even though I wanted to)

I never said **that** - (I did not say that thing which you think I said)

Barriers to Communication (Speaker):

Communication barriers encompass various obstacles that hinder effective communication, thereby impeding the transmission and reception processes. These barriers may arise from issues related to both the speaker and the listener. Numerous factors can undermine proper communication. Let's explore some instances where the speaker bears responsibility for these barriers.

- Firstly, the quantity of information presented can become a hindrance if it is extensive and lacks clarity and precision. In such cases, the receiver may fail to grasp all the intended information.

- Secondly, an excess of information, leading to a message that is intricate and incomprehensible, poses a significant barrier to effective communication.

- In the context of a presentation, it is crucial for the speaker to follow a predetermined order, ensuring that the information is presented logically. Failure to do so may result in the listener not comprehending the significance of the information.

- Moreover, if the speaker himself is unfamiliar with the information being conveyed and cannot address any doubts raised by the listener, it leads to ineffective communication.

- Lastly, a speaker lacking experience in articulating thoughts effectively can inadvertently create an invisible barrier between himself and the listener. It is essential for speakers to be mindful of these potential barriers to foster successful communication.

- Written communication can pose comprehension challenges if the handwriting is illegible. In the past, doctors were advised to write drug names legibly, and later, the government mandated writing medication names in uppercase to prevent misinterpretation by pharmacists. The advent of computers has significantly reduced these issues. Nevertheless, errors in dispensing still occur with handwritten prescriptions.

A young woman arrived at the emergency room in an unconscious and convulsing state. Upon inquiry, it was revealed that she had been prescribed tablets for abdominal bloating. When the resident requested the prescription, a handwritten note was presented, indicating Tab. Dimol 2 tablets thrice daily for 2 days. Unfortunately, the doctor's handwriting proved illegible.

The patient's husband then showed the tablets to the resident, revealing they were Daonil tablets. It's important to note that while Dimol is Simethicone, an anti-flatulent tablet, Daonil is Glimepiride, an anti-diabetic medication.

The pharmacist, relying on the unclear prescription, dispensed Tab Daonil 2 tablets thrice daily, leading to a catastrophic outcome—severe hypoglycemia (low blood sugar) and unconsciousness in the patient.

This tragic incident stemmed from the doctor's indecipherable handwriting.

Overcoming Communication Barriers

- To effectively overcome communication barriers, speakers must establish a meaningful connection with their audience. This involves employing appropriate non-verbal communication, such as simple gestures and facial expressions like a smile.

- Utilizing straightforward language and constructing short sentences are vital. Clarity is key, especially when addressing an audience unfamiliar with the language used. In such cases, employing the local vernacular can enhance understanding.

- Cultural disparities may also impede communication. While eye contact is encouraged in Western cultures, it might be perceived as disrespectful in some Eastern countries like China. Awareness of these cultural differences is crucial to avoid misunderstandings.

- Regularly gauging the audience's comprehension is essential. Speakers should observe body language and non-verbal cues of the listener / audience.

- The speaker should frequently pause while speaking / presenting and pose questions to assess if the listener / audience is understanding the message conveyed.

- Encouraging the listener / audience to ask questions is another method to overcome barriers to communication.

- Finally, the speaker should endeavor to sum up what he said in a couple of sentences. This can encapsulate his whole message and make it comprehensible to the listener.

- As far as possible, the speaker should steer clear of jargons, slang words and acronyms or abbreviations in his speech, which a section of the audience may not understand. When speaking to a lay audience, the use of technical words should be avoided. This becomes more important when a medical practitioner or a nurse is speaking to a patient or to his family member.

In my role as the Chief of Medical Services at the hospital, a regular training program on Communication Strategies in the Workplace was conducted. This initiative, jointly organized by the Quality and HR departments, catered to various hospital staff. The driving forces behind this program were the hospital's CEO, Ms. Gracy Mathai, and COO, Mr. Saji Mathew. Frequently, I was engaged as a resource person for these training sessions.

The program eventually expanded to include doctors and all new hires during the onboarding process. It encompassed formal presentations and role-playing sessions. Participants were tasked with assuming the roles of both a patient and a healthcare provider. This hands-on approach aimed to underscore the critical importance of effective communication in a healthcare setting.

Listening.

Just as verbal communication is an important part of speaking, listening is an equally important and essential part of communication that renders a communication complete and effective. It is the ability to receive and interpret the messages conveyed accurately and effectively. A distinction should be made between *hearing* and *listening*. Hearing is the perception of the sound by the ear, just as we hear the traffic sounds, ambient noise, birds chirping etc. But listening is an active skill which consists of five different distinct components. They are:

Receiving : The conveyed words are properly heard and their meaning and import recognized. It is the first stage in listening where the person has to *attend to* what is being said.

Understanding : This is the next stage in the listening process where the listener comprehends what is being said by the speaker. What the speaker intends in his message and what the listener understands should be the same.

Evaluating : The listener decides on the meaning of what he heard and understood from the speaker's words. He judges the value of the message. He uses his logical brain to analyze what he understood. What did the speaker intend, was the speaker biased in his opinion, was he being truthful in his statements, was he factual and so on. Does the listener trust the speaker? Is the speaker being hypocritical in his statements? Often, the listener evaluates the speaker based on <u>what is not said rather than what is said</u>. These are evaluated by the listener in his mind after he understands the speaker's words.

Remembering : The listener must retain the message for proper evaluation and response.. For this the listener should have been attentive from the beginning.

Responding : This is the final stage where the listener provides a feedback on the content of what he heard. It could be a verbal response or a non-verbal response. A verbal response is in the form of a question or a doubt raised by the listener. A non-verbal response can be in the form a nodding of the head, a smile, a frown, grimacing, or a rolling of the eyes indicating non agreement with the speaker. This also gives the speaker the indication that his message was understood and evaluated properly.

Surprisingly, leaders, especially executives and managers, dedicate more time to listening than speaking. Unfortunately, effective listening skills are rare among individuals. Leaders cultivate active listening skills to gain popularity with their followers.

Barriers to Communication (Listener):

Barriers arising from the listener's shortcomings are a significant concern and can stem from various causes. Reception issues may arise from:

- <u>Physical causes</u> like ambient noise and distractions in the room or outside. If the room where the communication is taking place is not sound proof, outside noises may interfere with communication. Noise can be due to voices outside, traffic in a nearby street, noise due to equipment, machinery and so on. Uncomfortable room temperature or poor seating arrangements may also distress the listener.
- <u>Physiological factors</u>, originating from the listener, like hearing impairments, which can impact message reception.

- <u>Psychological 'noise'</u> or <u>Attitudinal barriers</u> are due to inattentiveness or hostility of the listener, fear, egocentrism, or prejudice.
- Problems can be due to the <u>Receiver's comprehension</u>. He may not understand technical terms or jargon or slang used by the speaker. Cultural differences further contribute to comprehension difficulties. Listeners from the East may not understand the slang or jargon used by speakers from the West.

During our hospital's communication training, a key role-playing exercise involved the demonstration of the *'Chinese Whispers'* game, known as *'Telephone'* in American terminology. In this activity, a brief passage or story was initially shared with one person, who then whispered it into the ear of the next participant. This process continued through five or six individuals, each passing on the story to their neighbor through whispers. The final participant was tasked with repeating what they had heard. Frequently, the version recounted by the last person differed significantly, becoming a distorted variation of the original story.

This exercise effectively highlighted the pitfalls in listening and the potential errors introduced during the transmission of information from one person to another.

How can one be a good listener.

The most important requisite in interest in what is being said. The main needs for a good listener are:

- Firstly, a person must be willing to listen, motivated to understand, and evaluate the information presented.
- A good listener approaches the conversation with an open, unbiased mind, occupying a front-row seat for optimal engagement.
- Attention to the speaker's non-verbal cues is crucial for discerning message nuances.
- Complete focus on the speaker is maintained, avoiding distractions such as mobile phones or observing other audience members.
- Non-verbal responses, like nodding, smiling, or occasional eye contact, are employed to encourage the speaker appropriately.

How Speakers Can Enhance Listening Experience

- A proficient speaker must comprehend their audience and demonstrate empathy towards them, ensuring undivided attention.
- He should avoid using complex words and phrases. He should tailor his presentation to suit the needs of his audience and adjust his language appropriate to the educational standards of the audience.
- Articulating thoughts clearly, audibly, and in a modulated voice, the speaker ensures everyone can follow, steering clear of monotony.
- A good speaker should pay attention to the verbal and non-verbal cues of the audience which tells him whether the

audience is interested, confused, or bored.

- Thorough preparation and expertise on the subject equip the speaker to handle any arising questions confidently.
- Keeping presentations concise, engaging, and dynamic, the speaker achieves this by varying tone and incorporating anecdotes or quotes.

How can we be better communicators in the Workplace.

Communication is a skill that can be cultivated through consistent and deliberate practice. To develop this skill, one must engage in regular practice, considering the following guidelines:

- <u>Clarity is Key</u>. Clearly express your thoughts, using simple, straightforward language that everyone can grasp. Keep your messages concise, avoiding intricate sentences and complex vocabulary. Don't show off your vocabulary and language proficiency while communicating with your staff and students.
- <u>Tailor your communication</u> to your audience, steering clear of uncommon abbreviations and acronyms, as their meanings can vary in different contexts.
- <u>Speak slowly</u> and take care to articulate the words carefully considering diverse socioeconomic and educational backgrounds among employees.
- Use the <u>local vernacular</u> if it facilitates better understanding.

- <u>Illustrate with Examples.</u> While giving a speech, whenever possible flavor your communication with examples and anecdotes. Enrich your communication with relevant examples and anecdotes, adding a dynamic quality to speeches.
- <u>Embrace Open-Mindedness.</u> Welcome suggestions from employees, valuing their ideas regardless of perceived

significance. Studies reveal that businesses fostering employee satisfaction yield a 23% increase in profits.

- <u>Reinforce Important Messages.</u> reiterate crucial information to emphasize its importance.
- If you are presenting an important topic or piece of information, <u>supplement your communication with visual aids</u> like charts or slides as it enhances the understanding by the audience.
- <u>Solicit Feedback</u>. Request feedback during presentations to ensure clarity and understanding.
- <u>Be mindful of your non-verbal communication</u> and cues. It is important to give the proper non-verbal cues and exhibit appropriate body language while communicating. Steer clear of negative body language like avoiding eye contact, crossing of arms, frowning, or fiddling with a pen or paperweight on the table. These convey to the person that you are not interested in the person or what he is speaking.
- <u>Individual Focus</u>: When engaging with someone one-on-one, eliminate distractions such as mobile phones or ongoing events. Maintain focus during conversations, avoiding multitasking.
- <u>Refrain from interrupting</u> when others are speaking. Offer undivided attention and genuine interest, listening not just to respond but to understand. Try to comprehend the emotion behind the words of the speaker. Do not be judgmental regarding the speaker while you are listening.

One afternoon, the nurse in charge urgently summoned the resident on duty to assess a patient who had abruptly entered a stuporous state, displaying symptoms of sweating and disorientation. The patient, diagnosed with diabetes, adhered to a thrice-daily regimen of regular insulin, accompanied by corresponding blood glucose monitoring.

The concerning incident transpired following the administration of the pre-lunch insulin dose by a recently appointed nurse. Upon the resident's swift arrival at the patient's bedside, a startlingly low blood sugar level of 36 mg/dL was discovered. The resident promptly prescribed an intravenous infusion of 25% glucose to normalize the blood sugar, successfully averting a potential catastrophe and facilitating the patient's full recovery.

A subsequent examination into the root cause of the hypoglycemic episode revealed a miscommunication. The new nurse, seeking guidance from the consultant, conveyed the patient's pre-lunch blood sugar level over the telephone. While the consultant, occupied with driving, recommended a 16-unit injection of regular insulin, the nurse misconstrued this as "sixty units" and administered a potentially harmful dose, leading to the hypoglycemic crisis.

This incident serves as a vivid and authentic illustration of communication breakdown within a hospital setting. The nurse could have prevented the calamity by clarifying and confirming the instruction as "one-six units." Similarly, the consultant could have conveyed the instruction numerically, mitigating the risk of misinterpretation. Emphasizing the importance of a 'read back policy,' where received instructions are repeated before execution, becomes evident from this occurrence.

Email Etiquette.

Email etiquette encompasses the principles and behaviors one should observe when communicating through emails. It is widely understood that the tone and content of an email sent to a friend or family member would differ significantly from one addressed to a professional colleague, manager, or supervisor. Adhering to proper email etiquette reflects both professionalism and efficiency. Here are some guidelines for composing or responding to emails:

- Always have a clear and brief subject line. It should mention what your email is about or what you are replying to.
- Utilize standard fonts such as Georgia, Times New Roman, or Arial; **bold** or *italics* should be used judiciously only to emphasize key points.
- Reserve personal email addresses for informal communication and employ professional email addresses for official purposes.
- Maintain brevity in your message; introduce yourself and the email's topic early on. Use straightforward language, avoid unnecessary details, and maintain a professional tone.
- Use the proper form for addressing the person. Address the recipient appropriately, using formal salutations like "*Dear Mr. Jones*" or "*Good morning, John*," depending on the context.
- Conclude the email with courteous phrases like '*Sincerely*,' '*Kind regards*,' 'Thank you,' '*Hoping to hear from you soon*,' or '*With best wishes*.'
- Refrain from writing in all capital letters, as it can be perceived as rude and akin to shouting.
- Clearly mention any attachments in the email and consider compressing them when possible.
- Always proof read your email before hitting the send button to catch errors. Be careful never to send an email when you are

upset or angry with a person. In such cases, save your mail in 'Drafts' and revisit them after a day or two for revisions.

- Exercise caution with the use of emojis, especially in formal correspondence. Avoid slang and acronyms that the recipient may not comprehend.

- Commit to responding to emails within 12-24 hours as a matter of politeness and professionalism; never ignore an email.

- Be careful when you use the 'Cc' or 'Bcc' button to copy the mail to others. While replying, be vary of using the 'Reply' and 'Reply All' buttons.

Presentations.

Presentations are often a source of anxiety for many individuals. In an organizational context, managers and senior staff must possess effective public speaking and presentation skills to thrive in their careers. The ability to address an audience distinguishes a leader from the average person, making it advantageous for personal development. This skill is attainable through dedicated training and effort.

To enhance public speaking and presentation skills, consider the following strategies:

- Know who your audience are. The speech or presentation should be tailored according to the audience. Speaking to a group of school or college students is entirely different from speaking to a group of professionals. The content of the presentation, the language and the visual aids will be totally different in both the cases. Understanding your audience beforehand is crucial for effective preparation.

- Preparation for the presentation should be done well in advance and the speech should be rehearsed repeatedly so as to develop a confidence in presenting it. Essential information that is to be conveyed must be gathered and the presentation built around it. Structure your presentation with a 10% introduction, 75% content, and 15% conclusion. Repeated rehearsal ensures a polished delivery.

- *When you begin, tell the audience what you are going to tell them, then tell them and then them what you told them.* Organize your content using headings and subheadings to aid audience comprehension.

- Be thorough in your subject knowledge and anticipate questions at the end of the presentation.

- Always conclude your presentation with a concise summary of key points using bullet points.
- Effective Use of Visual Aids: Utilize visual aids, such as PowerPoint slides, sparingly. Avoid clutter, and don't read directly from the screen. Use slides as complementary tools, not as the main focus.
- Incorporate anecdotes, stories, and occasional humor to engage your audience, but maintain balance. But don't overdo it.
- Be professionally dressed depending on the occasion. Be well groomed. Stand erect. Do not slouch. Do not lean on the podium or table for support. Don't turn your back on the audience when you present the slides but stand to one side.
- Watch your body language. Make eye contact with members of the audience, but do not stare at one or two persons only.
- Vary the tone of your presentation and use inflections in your speech to break the monotony of the presentation. Occasionally, pause for emphasis. Repeat certain sentences to drive in the point.
- Ensure your voice reaches every corner of the room. Speak in short sentences, avoiding verbosity. Use pauses for emphasis, repeat key points, and vary your tone to prevent monotony.
- Be mindful of your body language, giving positive non-verbal cues that reinforce your message.
- Conclude with an invitation for questions and feedback. Respond politely and respectfully, even to challenging comments.

In the pursuit of career success, continuously acquiring and refining skills is essential. Acquiring new skills and honing them from time to time should be the intention of every employee in an organization. This will ensure his continued advancement in the organization. Employees should focus on developing their skill portfolios to ensure ongoing advancement within the organization.

"Effective communication is the cornerstone of patient-centered care" – **Critical Conversations in Healthcare.**

3. Healthcare Dialogue - DOCTOR-(NURSE) PATIENT COMMUNICATION

"The patient will never care how much you knew, until they know how much you care"
– Terry Canale.

Medicine encompasses both art and science. The scientific facet involves diagnosing and treating diseases, a proficiency acquired during a medical student's training. However, the art of practicing medicine must be nurtured, comprising skills such as communication, interpersonal relations, leadership, problem-solving, and conflict resolution. These skills, pivotal for a healthcare practitioner, evolve through practice and training, defining a doctor's likability to patients.

Notably, a significant number of complaints against healthcare professionals arise from deficient communication and interpersonal skills. Insufficient communication skills can lead to patient discontent, emphasizing that a doctor's interaction with the patient hinges on trust, openness, and mutual respect.

Why should doctors and nurses have good communication skills?

- <u>Positive Impression:</u> A healthcare professional's strong interpersonal skills leave a favorable impact on patients and their families. Patients often gauge a doctor's efficacy through their perceived 'bedside manners.'
- <u>Effective Information Exchange:</u> Good communication skills help the doctor and the nurse to exchange information with the patient and his family members successfully.
- <u>Inclusive Decision-Making:</u> Healthcare practitioners with adept interpersonal and communication skills involve patients

in decisions regarding disease treatment.

During my residency in northern India, where Hindi is the vernacular language, a peculiar incident unfolded. Despite having studied Hindi in school and college, our proficiency in its colloquial use was insufficient.

In a separate department, a fellow resident was assigned by the Professor to conduct blood tests on a fifteen-year-old boy from a nearby village, who was illiterate. The resident, armed with a syringe, approached the boy and spoke in a hushed tone. Suddenly, the boy screamed and bolted out of the room in terror, causing a momentary commotion.

The cause of the boy's panic soon became apparent. The resident had whispered, "*Tumhara khoon karna hai*," which in Hindi has a dual meaning: 'blood' and 'murder.' Due to his limited Hindi knowledge, he unintentionally conveyed, "*I am going to murder you*" instead of the intended "*I am going to test your blood*" No wonder the boy was in a state of panic!

Despite being advised to utilize an interpreter when communicating with villagers in Hindi, my friend, in haste, neglected this guidance and relied on his basic Hindi skills, leading to a humorous predicament. We all shared a hearty laugh at the incident.

This anecdote underscores the crucial role of effective communication in a hospital setting.

What are the advantages of good Doctor (Nurse)-Patient communication?

- A healthcare professional with strong interpersonal and communication skills encourages patients to share relevant personal information, aiding in diagnosis and treatment.
- The patient tends to follow the advice given by the doctor / nurse and are compliant with regard to the treatment and follow up.
- This instills confidence in patients, positively impacting their mental health and morale.
- Satisfaction with treatment reduces conflicts and malpractice complaints among patients and their families.
- The doctors and nurses also feel less stressed when the patients are compliant and satisfied with the treatment and thus this creates greater job satisfaction for the health care professionals.

What are the prevalent challenges that can hinder effective doctor-patient communication?

Many problems may occur during the career of a doctor / nurse which can adversely affect their communication with the patients.

A woman undergoing treatment for Rheumatoid Arthritis was admitted to the hospital due to intense vomiting and mouth ulcers. She had a prescription for Methotrexate tablets at a **weekly** dosage of 15 mg. Unfortunately, neither the doctor nor the pharmacist stressed the importance of taking methotrexate on a weekly basis. Consequently, the patient mistakenly consumed the tablets **daily**, leading to an overdose and subsequent adverse reactions.

- The demanding workload, especially during internship and residency, induces mental and physical stress, affecting how doctors/nurses engage with patients.
- Some practitioners exhibit avoidance behavior, sidestepping patient, and family queries, leading to dissatisfaction. Certain doctors discourage patients from asking numerous questions, creating a barrier to open communication.
- Patients, grappling with illness-related anxiety and fear, may doubt the veracity of the doctor's information.
- Unrealistic patient expectations can make doctors defensive, straining the doctor-patient relationship.
- The fear of verbal or physical abuse from the patient or their relatives and the fear of litigation, causes the doctor / nurse to dread freely and openly communicating with the patient or their relatives.
- The assertiveness of modern patients, armed with half-baked online knowledge, often renders open discussions futile.
- Patients may reject medical advice due to factors such as dietary habits, cultural differences, or lifestyle preferences.
- Poor patient comprehension may result from low educational status, ignorance, or mental disturbances linked to the illness.

During my consultancy at a large teaching hospital in southern India, a notable incident occurred in the bustling emergency room. A pregnant woman, referred from a nearby town in a critical state, arrived one day. The woman was in labor, and her blood pressure was dangerously low. Upon examination, the Gynecologist determined that the baby had died in utero. Despite the challenging circumstances, the medical team successfully delivered the deceased baby, saving the mother and restoring her blood pressure to normal.

Despite the loss of the baby, the fact that the mother was well brought solace to the woman's husband. Regrettably, a junior intern, who had assisted in the delivery, made a seemingly harmless but careless remark to the patient's brother. The intern suggested that had they arrived a bit earlier, the baby could have been saved. This innocent comment set off a series of events. The patient's relatives stormed the referring hospital in the nearby town, vandalizing it and threatening the Gynecologist for not referring the patient in time to potentially save the baby.

This incident underscored the profound impact that thoughtless and improper communication can have in a healthcare setting, causing considerable turmoil.

Strategies to Enhance Doctor/Nurse-Patient Communication

1. Enhancing Communication Skills: This is the most important strategy that doctors and nurses should adopt. Unfortunately, communication skills are not consistently part of medical or nursing training. While some medical schools now integrate this into their curriculum for students and residents, it remains crucial for healthcare professionals to continually refine their speaking and listening abilities. The art of conveying empathy, especially when delivering difficult news, is vital and requires development. (See Chapter 4 on *Breaking Bad News*). A doctor should always be mindful of his non-verbal cues while interacting with the patient or their family members.

When necessary, providing instructions in a written format is essential. Demonstrating the use of equipment like inhalers or nebulizers is equally important to ensure proper understanding by both patients and their families.

2. Collaborative Communication : This is a term which is used to indicate a two way communication between the doctor and the patient. This leads to a discussion of the outcomes and preferences regarding the treatment of the patient. All the concerns of the patient are addressed and the best outcome is ensured. Decision making is shared between the doctor and the patient. This leads to better compliance and trust between the doctor and the patient. Thus the treatment of the patient is tailored to the needs of the patient and the situation.

3. Handling Conflicts: Patients, dealing with illness, may experience confusion, frustration, anger, depression, or grief. Timely addressing of these emotions prevents potential conflicts that could strain the doctor-patient or nurse-patient relationship. An empathetic approach by healthcare professionals contributes to mitigating conflicts and soothing patient emotions.

4. Acknowledging Patient Beliefs Patients hold diverse beliefs, including cultural and religious differences. Some may prefer alternative treatments such as Ayurveda or Homeopathy. Effective communication by healthcare providers is crucial in convincing patients of the most suitable treatment for them. This understanding is essential in resolving potential conflicts arising from varying belief systems.

Practical Tips and Etiquette in Patient Care

Practicing essential skills and finesse when interacting with patients and their families in healthcare settings is crucial. Let's delve into some practical tips and etiquettes:

- Always knock before entering a patient's room.
- Greet the patient by name and introduce yourself.
- Maintain eye contact during conversations. Speak in the patient's language if you can. It gives him the feeling that you are 'concerned' about him.
- Ensure privacy by closing doors or screens during discussions.
- Sit at eye level with the patient, whether in a clinic or a hospital room.
- As far as possible, use simple language and avoid using technical terms while speaking to the patient. Always confirm whether the patient understands what you say.
- Allow the patient to speak without interruption; gently guide them back to the discussion if he tends to stray from the subject.
- Avoid turning your back on the patient while you are with him.
- Show concern, empathy, and sensitivity to the patient's feelings.
- Use simple diagrams, sketches, pictures, or videos to explain to the patient details of the diagnosis and treatment. Always ask the patient if he understands what you say. Answer all his questions however silly they seem to be.
- Address patient queries about diet, exercise, or other concerns patiently and without being judgmental.
- Include family members in discussions when appropriate,

ensuring patient confidentiality when needed.

- Be receptive to the patient's perspective; take time to patiently explain the pros and cons of your view, especially when fear or anxiety influences their questions.
- When assessing the patient's understanding of the disease and situation, use open-ended questions.

Some Aspects of Non-Verbal Communication in Healthcare.

Patients and their families often discern non-verbal signals from doctors and nurses, interpreting them in various ways. Consequently, healthcare professionals must exercise caution in conveying non-verbal cues during patient interactions. These cues, reflecting the doctor's emotions and attitudes, are frequently involuntary, and the doctor may be unaware of their display.

Elements such as tone of speech, eye contact, and facial expressions are observed by patients. Even the doctor's silence can be particularly significant to patients. Facial expressions, like a serious demeanor, a frown, or a smile, often communicate more than words. Younger and more educated patients tend to be more adept at interpreting these non-verbal cues.

Computers and Medical Communication

The integration of computers has transformed the dynamics of communication between healthcare professionals and patients. As doctors increasingly rely on computers to document their findings, there is a noticeable reduction in direct patient interaction. The diminished eye contact and the doctor's frequent shift of attention towards the computer can create discomfort for the patient.

In a comprehensive study involving 700 Orthopedic surgeons and 807 patients, it was revealed that 75% of the surgeons believed their communication was satisfactory. However, only 21% of the interviewed patients expressed genuine satisfaction with their doctor's communication.

Another study highlighted the influence of patient demographics on communication, revealing that factors such as age, gender, and educational background played a role. Notably, doctors tended to communicate less with economically disadvantaged and educationally less privileged patients.

To establish trust when inputting data into a computer during a clinic visit, doctors should consider the following guidelines:

- The doctor should refrain from taking notes while the patient is initially speaking, waiting until the patient completes his opening statement.
- If possible, data entry into the computer should be postponed until after the patient has left the consultation room.
- If necessary to enter information during the session, the doctor should seek the patient's permission before doing so.
- The doctor should maintain face-to-face interaction and eye contact when actively listening to the patient.
- The examination of the patient should commence only after the patient has concluded presenting their symptoms and

concerns.

What patients expect from their doctors

Patients expect doctors to reassure them. Patients like doctors who encourage them to ask questions. When laboratory results are accessible, patients expect detailed discussions from their doctors, explaining the implications. Interestingly, one study found that the patients' perception differed when the doctor sat with them and discussed the details. They felt that the doctor *spent more time* with them while sitting rather than while standing. Patients do not appreciate being judged by their healthcare practitioners. They value doctors who actively engage them in the decision-making process.

"Unacceptable Behaviour" by the doctor.

Certain attitudes and behaviors exhibited by doctors are perceived by patients as 'unacceptable and rude.' Some of these behavior patterns include:

- Any conduct which violates patient's rights.
- Verbally abusing or displaying angry behavior in the presence of patients.
- Showing disrespect for any religion or exhibiting religious bias.
- Making negative comments about a colleague or nurse.
- Expressing unacceptable remarks about the hospital or its management.
- Criticizing a patient's behavior in the presence of others.
- Acting rudely towards nurses or other paramedics in the patient's view.
- Making derogatory comments about alternative systems of medicine. Mocking or making any sort of disparaging remarks in the presence of the patient
- Displaying offensive facial expressions.
- Ignoring the patient's questions and doubts and not addressing them adequately.
- Smoking and consuming alcohol in the workplace, behaviors frowned upon by patients who are highly sensitive to such conduct from doctors or nurses.
- Doctor-nurse quarrels are unacceptable to patients and their families.
- Disrespect towards female patients is intolerable to patients and their families.
- Making statements like '*I am overworked*,' '*I am fed up*,' '*I am busy, I have no time now for you*,' '*We have a shortage of staff*

in this hospital' are phrases patients do not appreciate hearing from doctors or nurses.

What Defines a 'Good' Doctor or Nurse

Patients hold distinct views on what makes a good doctor. In the past, doctors and nurses were revered, but the rise of consumerism and the corporatization of medical practice has shifted patient and public perceptions. Patients form their own criteria for determining a 'good' doctor or nurse, including:

- A good doctor or nurse is one who empathizes and is sensitive to the feelings of the patient and the family. This is more so when the healthcare practitioner has to communicate bad news to them.
- A good doctor must establish trust in the patient by telling him the reasoning behind the treatment and its strategies.
- A doctor with an updated office with all the new equipment and technology to support the diagnosis and treatment of the illness is appreciated by the patient and his family.
- Fostering positive relationships with staff, including nurses, technicians, and other hospital personnel.
- Commitment to patient care, honesty, openness, and respect for patient wishes.
- Being well-trained and skilled in their area of expertise, garnering respect from patients and families.

The journey to becoming a successful doctor or nurse should commence during medical/nursing education. Teachers and mentors play a pivotal role in shaping the behavior and attitude of medical and nursing students during their education and internships. Communication and interpersonal skills are as vital as technical proficiency in the study of medicine and nursing. The curriculum should adapt to modern technological advancements, ensuring a balance between human touch and the ever-evolving landscape of technology and science in medical practice.

"The practice of medicine is an art, not a trade; a calling, not a business; a calling in which your heart will be exercised equally with your head"
- Sir William Osler.

5. Conveying Unpleasant Truths - BREAKING BAD NEWS

"Though it be honest, it is never good to bring bad news"
- William Shakespeare[1]

One of the most challenging responsibilities for a physician entering the field of medicine is the task of delivering unwelcome news to patients or their families. Regrettably, this vital skill is often overlooked in medical school curricula, causing many residents to initially shy away from this duty. Patients vary, but most would appreciate a candid and compassionate explanation when faced with unfortunate news, whether it pertains to a severe illness, a progressively debilitating condition, or the loss of a loved one. Physicians frequently find themselves managing the family's emotional responses to the news they convey.

The art of breaking bad news can be acquired through training and practice. When executed adeptly, this skill can alleviate the distress experienced by both the patient and their family. Medical education and training periods should include instruction for residents and nursing staff on mastering this delicate communication skill. Proficiency in communication is imperative to effectively deliver distressing news. Interestingly, it has been observed that inadequate communication skills, rather than medical negligence, underlie many medical litigation cases.

Most medical schools and universities worldwide have incorporated soft skill training into their updated curriculum. This inclusion has significantly enhanced essential skills such as communication, delivering difficult news, empathy, attitude, and interpersonal relationships within the medical and nursing communities.

---

1. https://www.overallmotivation.com/quotes/william-shakespeare-quotes/

Definition : <u>*Bad news is undesirable, troublesome or dangerous news that drastically alters the patient's view of his or her future*</u>. Learning about a cancer diagnosis, muscular dystrophy in a child, an incurable heart disease in a family provider, or dementia in a 50-year-old academician can be devastating to the patient.

The ABCDE Mnemonic for Breaking Bad News

A straightforward mnemonic, ABCDE, proposed by Rabow & McPhee, can guide practitioners in the step-by-step process of delivering difficult news to patients or their relatives. [1].

Advance Preparation : The physician must adequately prepare before delivering distressing news. Thoroughly reviewing the patient's case file, including the diagnosis, clinical features, and laboratory results, is crucial. Being capable of addressing queries from the patient or their family is equally important.

Moreover, the physician should cultivate mental and emotional readiness to communicate confidently. Meetings with the patient or their relatives should occur in a well-furnished, comfortable room, free from distractions such as mobile phones or calls. Ensure that the individuals involved are comfortably seated before initiating the conversation; avoid delivering bad news while they are standing.

Acquiring background knowledge about the patient and their family beforehand is beneficial. This knowledge can help the physician anticipate potential emotional responses, such as outbursts, depression, or panic reactions. Overall, meticulous preparation ensures a smoother and more empathetic delivery of difficult information. The physician should be mentally and emotionally prepared to face the patient / relatives with confidence. The conversation should be uninterrupted and any distractions like the mobile phone or telephone calls should be avoided.

Build a Relationship : It is beneficial for physicians to gauge the patient's knowledge and desired level of information about their illness. Some patients, driven by fear, may not be prepared to absorb detailed information and may require a more curated version of the news. Others may seek comprehensive details, including laboratory results, biopsy findings, prognosis, and treatment plans. It is crucial to discern the patient's preferences before engaging them in conversation.

Incorporating family members into the discussion is an option if the patient is amenable, especially if emotional support is desired. However, this decision should respect the patient's discretion and confidentiality, and the physician must assess the situation beforehand.

Always introduce yourself before beginning the discussion. Any resident, trainee or nurse present should also be introduced and permitted to stay with the permission of the patient.

When delivering unfortunate news, commence by expressing empathy, such as saying, *'I regret to inform you of challenging news.'* Or *'I am sorry to bring bad news'*. This preliminary statement prepares both the patient and family members for the forthcoming information.

Decide the extent of information to share, preferably with the patient's case record on hand for fact verification. Emotional responses may surface during the conversation, and the physician should respond empathetically.

In certain cultural contexts, like Eastern cultures such as India, patients or their family members may not wish to be physically touched during emotional interviews. Awareness of cultural diversity is essential; while some cultures may find comfort in physical gestures like placing hands on shoulders or gentle pats on the back, others may perceive this differently. Physicians should navigate these cultural nuances with sensitivity.

Communication : Before delivering difficult news, it is preferable to inquire about the patient and relatives' existing knowledge of the illness and situation. The strategy of "Ask before telling" is endorsed by many experts.

Utilize simple and comprehensible language, and, if comfortable, the patient's vernacular. Consider the patient's educational level when providing information.

One should be careful not to use medical terms which the patient or the family members may not understand. Simple terms like *'cancer'*, *'death'*, *'disability'*, *'progress'* etc., should be used.

If needed, diagrams or sketches may be used as aids to make the patient understand the details. The patient should always be asked whether he understands what is being said. He may even be asked to repeat it in brief.

Avoid rushing through conversations; allow sufficient time for information absorption. If emotions surface, pause until recovery before continuing.

Questions should always be encouraged so that there are no lingering uncertainties at the end of the interview.

Conclude with a summary of the entire discussion in a couple of sentences. Assure the patient and relatives of your availability for further discussions or clarifications about the patient's illness or treatment.

Dealing with the patient's / family's reactions : While elucidating the details and information, the physician should keenly observe the body language of both the patient and their family members. This provides an opportunity to gauge their attitudes and level of acceptance toward the situation.

Expressing empathy is crucial; the physician can use phrases like *'I regret to inform you'* or *'unfortunately'.*

If confronted with a question for which the physician lacks an answer, honesty is paramount. It's advisable to admit not knowing and assure the patient, *'I will check and inform you.'* Transparency is key in delivering difficult news; patients must not perceive any attempt to conceal information.

Avoid criticizing colleagues or their treatment during the communication process. Critiques may negatively impact both the physician and the hospital, potentially leading to adverse consequences.

Encourage Emotions : It is suitable to provide realistic hope to the patient, avoiding the dissemination of false expectations. Do not give false hopes to the patient.

After delivering unfavorable news, it is entirely acceptable to inquire about the patient's emotional well-being.

If the patient seeks a second opinion or additional referrals, facilitate the necessary arrangements. Depending on requirements, other medical specialties may become part of the patient's overall care.

Schedule a follow up discussion to clear any doubts or queries that the patient or family members may harbor concerning the illness or its treatment.

Conveying news of Death

Informing family members about the death of a loved one or close relative is among the most challenging tasks a physician faces. This responsibility demands a certain level of training and expertise. Many residents hesitate to share news of a patient's death due to concerns about potential repercussions and emotional reactions. The ABCDE method, mentioned earlier, is also applicable when delivering the news of death. Additionally, consider the following tips:

- Establishing a good rapport with the deceased patient's relatives before delivering the news is crucial. Often, the physician overseeing the patient is the one responsible for conveying the message.
- Prepare what to say and have the case file ready, if necessary.
- Always verify the identity of the deceased and the relative(s) before initiating the conversation. Confirm that the relative is an adult. Excluding children from the discussion may be preferable.
- Introduce oneself and clarify one's role in patient management. While a senior team member should ideally deliver the news, it need not be the person who performed CPR or declared death.
- Deliver the news promptly and use explicit language, avoiding euphemisms. Instead of saying *"no more"* or *"passed away,"* use direct language like *"he died."*
- Refrain from conveying news of death over the phone. If no relative is present during the patient's death, identify yourself and summon the relative to the hospital. If the close relative is not on-site, confirm that you are speaking to an adult (not a child) before delivering the message.
- Ask the family to sit in a comfortable area before discussing

the matter.

- Assess whether the relative has any support and, if necessary, offer to call someone for them. A social worker may assist with further arrangements for the relatives.
- Avoid using inappropriate terms of consolation, such as 'He has lived a full life,' 'God needed him,' or 'His death was a blessing from his suffering.' Healthcare professionals should desist from such phrases.

In spite of these painful circumstances, the physician can provide moral support to the family by his presence and offering any help they may need in the form of arrangements and speeding up the procedures at the hospital.

"Better to have bad news that's true than good news we made up" - Eric Ries

6. The Art of Relating – INTERPERSONAL SKILLS

"The challenge that many people face while interacting with others is that they lack necessary interpersonal skills needed to be effective"
– Robert W Lucas.

Man is not an isolated entity. Throughout our lives, we must engage with a diverse array of individuals, each possessing unique characters, attitudes, and behaviors. This interaction is a requisite not only in our professional settings but also within our homes and broader society. Effectual interpersonal skills are imperative for fostering harmonious relationships with others be it the organization, our family or society at large. Ability to work in a group or team was mentioned as the most important skill needed in an organization by 60% of the employees.

Definition : Interpersonal Skill is defined as *"the skills one needs to use to communicate and interact with other people"*. Interpersonal skills, alternatively known as Social Skills, People Skills, Life Skills, Social Intelligence, or Soft Skills, encompass the abilities and strategies essential for effective communication and interaction. Regardless of one's role within an organization, these skills are indispensable for the seamless functioning of the entity, be it a family unit or a societal structure. Emotional intelligence is the bedrock of good interpersonal skills.

What are the benefits of Interpersonal Skills.

The benefits of interpersonal skills are multifaceted. They bolster trust and dependability, increasing the likelihood of professional advancement and fostering cooperative relationships in the workplace. The adept application of these skills minimizes conflict, averts complications, enhances work efficiency, and augments overall productivity. Positive outcomes extend to customer satisfaction and favorable feedback. Acquiring these skills through training is an invaluable asset for career progression.

In specialized fields like healthcare, impeccable interpersonal relationships are mandatory for those directly engaging with patients and their families. A robust rapport between healthcare providers, such as doctors and nurses, and patients often resolves minor issues and complaints, contributing to a smoother healthcare experience.

Within the family, adept interpersonal skills prove beneficial in averting family issues and facilitating effective parenting. Minor conflicts find resolution when partners maintain positive interpersonal relationships.

The essential interpersonal skills include Communication, Leadership, Problem Solving, and Decision Making. Effective communication involves active listening, a crucial component. Teamwork, negotiation, conflict resolution, and empathy are vital skills required not only in the workplace but also at home and in the community.

Developing Strong Interpersonal Skills

Before delving into enhancing interpersonal skills, self-assessment is crucial. Identifying existing skills and recognizing areas for improvement is essential for effective training. Some individuals may struggle with clear expression of ideas, poor listening, or difficulty presenting to a group. These shortcomings can be overcome through consistent practice and training. Recognizing our weaknesses is the first step towards self-improvement. Let's briefly explore how we can cultivate these skills.

Communication : Communication is a pivotal skill crucial for effective engagement in various settings, be it within an organization, at home, or in the community (See Chapter 2 on *'Communication'*). It encompasses both speaking and listening, where verbal and non-verbal elements hold equal significance. Improving vocabulary and honing spoken language proficiency are key aspects. Depending on the workplace, language proficiency may extend to English, one's vernacular, or another foreign language.

In addition to refining speaking and presentation abilities, mastering the art of active listening is imperative. In organizational leadership, individuals at the top spend more time listening than speaking. Active listening is a skill that demands dedicated practice.

Furthermore, expert negotiation and conflict resolution skills are natural by-products of strong communication abilities. The 7 C's of communication—*Clear, Concise, Concrete, Correct, Coherent, Complete*, and *Courteous*—serve as guiding principles for effective communication.

Positive Attitude : Cultivating a positive attitude is akin to completing half the task. Individuals with a positive mindset possess the ability to draw people towards them. This optimistic outlook inherently boosts self-confidence and diminishes workplace stress.

Being assertive, rather than aggressive, contributes to likability within the organization.

In a hospital where I served as the Chief of Medical Services, a situation arose when a consultant, accustomed to a room on the ground floor for nearly three years, needed to relocate. Another consultant from a different department required the same room. When the HR manager approached the consultant for the move to a different floor, he adamantly refused, firmly entrenched in his current comfort zone, thus sparking of a conflict.

The issue landed on my desk, necessitating my intervention. Contemplating the matter, I visited the consultant's room one afternoon, strategically avoiding the topic of relocation. Instead, I engaged him in a conversation about the book "*Angels and Demons*" by Dan Brown, which happened to be on his table. Steering clear of the room predicament, I offered him a selection of novels from my library.

Before departing, I casually mentioned the crowded and noisy ground floor corridor during peak hours, subtly hinting at a quieter environment without directly broaching the subject of the available room on the first floor. I left without explicitly discussing the alternative.

Within half an hour, the consultant called, inquiring about a different room. Proposing a first-floor room with minimal foot traffic and distractions, he eagerly accepted the suggestion.

Someone with a positive attitude tends to speak favorably about their organization and colleagues, refraining from negative remarks about past employers. Additionally, maintaining personal integrity and honesty is integral to a positive attitude. A person's reputation is evaluated based on these qualities.

Collaboration Effectively collaborating with colleagues and team members is a crucial interpersonal skill to cultivate. It involves aiding one another in tasks, sharing knowledge and expertise, and assisting with duties – all integral components of teamwork. Establishing positive relationships is fundamental for effective team building. Additionally, individuals should cultivate adaptability, flexibility, resilience, and a willingness to embrace changes and responsibilities assigned by management.

Emotional Regulation and Empathy: One should learn to control one's emotions while working in an organization. It is common to feel irritation or annoyance towards some co-workers, triggering frustration and anger. Yet, the ability to manage these emotions is paramount for fostering positive relationships within the organization.

Likewise, extending empathy towards colleagues facing genuine challenges, whether at work or home, significantly contributes to building and repairing strong relationships. Putting oneself in their shoes enhances understanding. Recognizing and acknowledging the efficiency and expertise of fellow co-workers, while seeking their assistance when needed, is imperative. Demonstrating genuine interest in the personal lives and concerns of colleagues is instrumental in cultivating camaraderie in the workplace. When you observe praiseworthy traits or habits in a colleague, remember to express sincere appreciation.

Cultural sensitivity is a vital element in effective interpersonal relationships, especially in the current era of globalization. Collaboration with individuals from diverse cultures worldwide is increasingly common. This is particularly crucial in the healthcare sector, where patients, representing various cultural backgrounds and societal strata, seek services. Building strong interpersonal connections is essential for effective communication within hospitals or clinics. Developing patience and tolerance becomes indispensable when interacting with individuals from different cultural backgrounds.

Leadership Skills : These skills are crucial for individuals aspiring to advance in their careers and are integral to effectively managing one's abilities. Inspiring, mentoring, and motivating others are essential leadership qualities that can be cultivated through learning. Leaders must be open to listening to all employees, regardless of their position, fostering confidence among the team. Effective communication, conflict resolution, negotiation, problem-solving, and decision-making are indispensable skills for any leader.

Consequently, refining interpersonal skills is essential not only in the workplace but also at home and in the community, as they are fundamental to every interaction. These skills can be developed through deliberate training and consistent practice.

"The Internet and online communication is the window into your world. But real life, in person communication / connection is the door"

- Rasheed Ogunlaru.

7. Continuity of Care – CLINICAL HANDOVER

"The very first requirement in a hospital is that it Should DO THE SICK NO HARM"
-Florence Nightingale

Communication is crucial in clinical settings, playing a vital role in the seamless operation of the healthcare system. A successful exchange of information among healthcare professionals demands an efficient and structured communication system. Failure to establish this may lead to errors, jeopardizing both patient safety and care quality. This is particularly significant during transitions of care when the responsibility for a patient's care shifts. Whether it's a nurse, doctor, or other personnel, each caregiver must provide accurate and up-to-date information to colleagues involved in the patient's care. Timely and precise communication is essential for effective patient care, emphasizing the importance of delivering the *right information to the right individuals at the right time*. The standardization of clinical handover procedures significantly enhances nursing handover practices.

Between 1995 and 2006 communication errors were cited as the leading cause of sentinel events reported to the Joint Commission in the USA. [5]. From Australia, it was reported that **11%** of the preventable adverse events out of about 25000 to 30000 patients was due to communication errors, whereas only **6%** were due to poor skill of the doctors. [5]. A recent study revealed that the weekly incidence of errors during clinical handover was 12 – 14% globally [7].

Definition : *"Clinical Handover is the transfer of professional responsibility and accountability for some or all aspects of care for a patient or a group of patients, to another person or professional group on a temporary or permanent basis."* [3].

Importance and Relevance of Clinical Handover

Clinical Handover holds significant importance in healthcare settings for several reasons:

- Enhanced Communication: Structured clinical handovers mitigate the risk of communication errors among healthcare personnel and organizations.
- Patient Safety and Quality Care: Effective clinical handovers contribute to the safety and quality of patient care.
- Continuity of Care: It plays a crucial role in maintaining seamless continuity of care for patients.
- Prevention of Adverse Events: Well-executed clinical handovers reduce the occurrence of adverse events, patient readmissions post-discharge, and enhance overall patient care outcomes.
- Risk Mitigation during Patient Transfer: Failure to conduct proper, structured clinical handovers during patient transfer can lead to errors in treatment.

More than fifty years ago, while I was in college preparing to enter medical school, a true event occurred. An elderly family priest sought consultation from his general practitioner for an inguinal hernia in his **left** groin. The family physician referred him to a larger center in the neighboring state of Tamil Nadu.

Upon examination, the surgeon scheduled the priest for surgery two days later. On the operating table, just before the anesthesiologist administered anesthesia, the surgeon, confirming the patient's name, signaled to proceed. The surgery took place, and the patient was transferred to the postoperative ICU. Upon regaining consciousness after the anesthesia wore off, the priest was dismayed to find a bandage in his **right** groin, opposite to the side where the hernia was located. An operation had been performed on the wrong side.

Upon investigation, it was discovered that two patients with similar names with inguinal hernias were scheduled for surgery on the same day. The other patient had a hernia on the **right** side. Due to miscommunication, a mix-up in patient identity occurred, leading to this unfortunate error.

This incident underscores the critical need for proper handover procedures and accurate patient identification, especially noting the side on which the surgery is intended. It transpired during a time when hospitals lacked structured clinical handover and identification processes.

When is Clinical Handover relevant?

Clinical handover is crucial in various situations, including:

- Shift changes between clinicians or nurses.
- Patient transfers within the same hospital, to another healthcare facility, or to a palliative care unit.
- Patient transitions from the Intensive Care Unit to a ward post-stabilization or following surgery.
- Management involving multiple teams, such as Neurology, Cardiology, and Physical Therapy, as seen in cases like stroke in a patient with valvular heart disease.
- Patient transfers for investigations like Angiography, MRI, or Endoscopy to different departments.
- Patient discharge, necessitating a handover to family members or the patient's caregiver.

In each scenario, those receiving patient information must possess essential details to ensure continuous and effective care. This transfer of information also signifies the transfer of _responsibility_ and _accountability_.

Methods Employed in Clinical Handover

Below is a concise overview of the different approaches:

- <u>Face-to-Face Handover:</u> This is the most common and effective method where patient details are verbally communicated to another healthcare professional.
- <u>Telephone Handover:</u> Used when a patient is moved to another care facility or hospital, or when transferred to a different consultant for additional treatment.
- <u>Written Orders:</u> This is the customary approach for conveying patient details during hospital discharge or when transferring to another healthcare institution.
- <u>Electronic Handover Tools or Systems:</u> Modern technological solutions allowing the seamless sharing of patient data with other facilities or consultants.

Where does the handover process take place?

In a hospital, the handover process typically involves a doctor or nurse, accompanied by another staff member. Handovers between nurses, junior doctors, and residents occur during shift changes. The incoming staff receives the handover information. When a patient is discharged, the handover is provided to a family member or caregiver.

Handovers can occur in the following locations:

- <u>At the patient's bedside:</u> This is considered the optimal method for transferring data between healthcare providers. It minimizes the chance of errors and ensures all patient updates are conveyed.
- <u>The common staff area or nursing station:</u> This location may be used when handing over a whole ward of patients during a shift change.

- <u>The hospital or clinic reception:</u> Handovers may occur in these areas when a patient is transferred between facilities, such as from one hospital to another.

Information Provided During A Handover

In essence, when transferring patient information, the following details must be conveyed to the recipient:

- The individual is correctly identified by name, identification number, and date of birth.
- A comprehensive clinical diagnosis, including present status, alerts, and a prognosis assessment, is provided.
- Specific clinical concerns, risk factors, chances for potential harm, warnings, and preventive strategies are communicated.
- A thorough medication history is essential, encompassing current medications, prescribed drugs, potential adverse reactions, dosing, and mode of administration.
- Relevant laboratory investigations are disclosed, emphasizing any abnormal results.
- A detailed plan for ongoing treatment, follow-up needs, and referrals, if required, is outlined.
- If the patient received blood or other transfusions, these instances are described, including any adverse effects.
- If the patient is infectious and can transmit the infection, this is clearly flagged as a warning.
- The name of the consultant responsible for transferring or discharging the patient is communicated.

Guidelines for Clinical Handover

The Western Australia Department of Health has issued crucial guidelines for handovers, outlined below: [3].

They are given below.

> Patient information must be communicated using simple and comprehensible language.

> Avoid the use of abbreviations during the handover process.

> The most senior clinician or nurse in the group should lead the process of transfer.

> Team members should clearly identify themselves to the recipients of the information.

> During a shift change, handovers should include all patients. Medical officers must cover newly admitted patients, those with special concerns, or critically ill individuals.

> Document the transfer process, including the handover time and date, relevant clinical information, and details of the giver and receiver.

> Handovers should occur face to face in the ward, patient bedside, or nursing station.

> When providing handovers or mentioning medications over the phone, insist that the recipient repeats the instructions. For numeric values, such as medication doses,

they should be articulated carefully, slowly, and in single digits (e.g., *"One-Five"* for **15** to avoid confusion with "fifty" - *Three-Two-Five* may be mentioned instead of **325**).

> Complete the discharge summary, containing all pertinent information, within 24 hours of the patient's discharge. Many hospitals provide the discharge summary at the time of discharge to ensure continuity of care at home.

The ISBAR Tool:

Enhancing Communication in Organizations.

The ISBAR tool serves as a structured communication tool applicable at all organizational levels. Initially devised by the US Navy to enhance clear and precise communication among nuclear submarines, it was developed to bolster safety in communication processes. In 2000, the US public health sector embraced this tool, and it has garnered approval from the World Health Organization for effective communication in healthcare institutions.

The acronym *'ISBAR'* simplifies the key components: *Identify*, *Situation*, *Background*, *Assessment*, and *Recommendation*. This mnemonic aids in remembering the critical aspects of communication. Presently, healthcare facilities worldwide have embraced ISBAR for interprofessional communication among healthcare providers. Its adoption contributes to enhanced operational excellence, fosters a collaborative environment, and elevates patient safety.

The ISBAR framework entails the following components:

1. **Identification**: The patient is identified through their Name, Date of Birth, and Medical Record Number. The person providing information must also self-identify, and the recipient of the information should likewise be identified. Relevant patient details, such as diagnosis, current clinical status, and medications, are communicated.

2. **Situation**: This segment elucidates the ongoing events. The reason for the current communication is highlighted, whether it pertains to the potential risk of delirium, falls, seizures, breathlessness, chest pain, or any other relevant concerns.

3. **Background:** The circumstances leading to the current situation are outlined in this section.

4. **Assessment:** This part encompasses the current evaluation

of the situation, including identified risks, recommended management strategies, tasks to be performed, and any further actions deemed necessary.

5. **Recommendation:** This final aspect suggests actions to rectify the problem, clarifying whether immediate intervention is imperative.

	ISBAR TOO	
I	**IDENTIFICATION**	The Patient identified Wh you calling f
S	**SITUATION**	What is pres calling
B	**BACKGROUND**	What issues Tell the Stor
A	**ASSESSMENT**	What do you present Wh
R	**RECOMMENDATION**	What should think should want from th

What are the advantages of incorporating ISBAR in a hospital setting?

The benefits of implementing ISBAR in a healthcare setting are briefly as follows.

- The person receiving the patient information is provided with comprehensive details, ensuring no crucial points are overlooked.
- Handovers become concise, focused, and precise.
- Both the communicator and the recipient gain a clear understanding of the situation, fostering confidence in proper management.
- Communication centers around the issues highlighted in the conversation.
- The entire process can be documented in the patient's case record in the same structured order of presentation.
- Patient safety is guaranteed through the effective transfer of information.

> **Identification** - Nurse (Mary, Staff Nurse, Medical Ward) contacts the duty resident, Dr. Smith, introducing herself and providing patient details: *"Mrs. Jane, 76 years old, in room 7725, is semi-conscious."*
>
> **Situation** - Describing the immediate scenario: *"She is sweating, groaning, barely rousable, and her blood sugar is 44 mg/dl."*
>
> **Background** - Providing contextual information: *"She is a diabetic on Regular Insulin thrice daily, with dosages adjusted based on blood sugar results. Tonight, she skipped dinner after her insulin dose."*
>
> **Assessment** - Nurse's analysis: *"I feel that her hypoglycaemia is causing the present symptoms."*
>
> **Recommendation** - Proposed actions: *"I am administering 25% glucose, followed by a Dextrose infusion.*
>
> *- Immediate doctor attendance is crucial. So please come immediately to see her.*
>
> *- Please inform the consultant for advice and further management.*
>
> *- I am planning an early breakfast for the patient."*

The ISBAR process is exemplified below through a midnight call from a nurse to the on-duty resident.

Initially, challenges may arise while incorporating ISBAR in a hospital setting, such as interruptions by the recipient with questions and the need for the communicator to repeat information. After conveying the information, proper documentation in the patient's case record is essential, a task simplified by ISBAR, especially with the availability of electronic systems. Various methods, including structured classes, role-play, videos, and other audiovisual aids, can facilitate training in Clinical Handover in a hospital setting.

In a hospital, the adoption of ISBAR for information transfer can be facilitated through the following approaches:

✓ New staff, including doctors and nurses, should undergo training in the tool's communication application.

✓ Printed stickers and posters strategically placed in the hospital can prompt the use of ISBAR.

✓ Stickers conveniently positioned next to telephones make the tool easily accessible for telephone communication.

✓ Pocket cards can be distributed to staff for quick reference.

✓ ISBAR stickers may be included in patient files. These may be incorporated into the inner side of the patient folder.

✓ The hospital should monitor and audit the use of ISBAR for communication, providing feedback to relevant stakeholders.

Barriers to Clinical Handover Process.

Hospital management occasionally encounters potential barriers in the clinical handover process that must be addressed by both management and senior staff members. Some of these barriers include:

- Resistance to change may arise when implementing a new handover policy in a hospital, impeding the process.
- Heavy workloads in certain hospitals can constrain the implementation of handover practices. Staff shortages and low health literacy pose challenges to the effective implementation of handover processes.
- Adequate training, particularly for newcomers, is essential for the widespread acceptance of the handover process among staff.
- Excessive time spent on clinical handover processes may lead to delays in patient care.
- The lack of proper information technology facilities in a hospital can hinder the efficient implementation of clinical handover processes.
- Cultural, language, and educational differences between patients and healthcare providers may act as barriers, particularly during the discharge process when informing patients and their families is crucial.

Global data indicates that proper clinical handover practices significantly reduce errors and miscommunication among healthcare providers. This, in turn, enhances patient safety, instills confidence in both patients and staff, and reduces the incidence of patient complaints and litigations.

"The most important thing in communication is hearing what isn't said"

– Peter Drucker.

7. Constructive Discord Handling - CONFLICT MANAGEMENT

"You can't shake hands with a clenched fist"
— Indira Gandhi

Conflicts are an inherent aspect of human existence, manifesting in various settings such as homes, offices, and communities. They range from individual disagreements to larger-scale disputes in companies or factories, resulting in strikes and diminished productivity. Annually, unresolved conflicts and low productivity cost American businesses nearly $359 billion (Kauth, 2020). The ramifications of conflicts extend beyond mere financial losses, encompassing physical, emotional, and psychological tolls.

Many individuals may avoid addressing conflicts due to personal or professional considerations. However, mastering effective conflict resolution is a crucial skill within any organization. Leaders frequently find themselves tasked with resolving diverse conflicts, refining this skill through continuous practice. Disagreements pose a challenge for management, as they can escalate into conflicts with potentially disastrous consequences if not promptly addressed.

Definition : *Conflict Resolution is the process or identifying, addressing, and resolving disagreements or disputes among employees in a professional setting.*

Causes of Workplace Conflicts

Numerous factors contribute to the emergence of conflicts in the workplace, affecting both individuals and teams. Let's explore some key contributors.

Poor Communication : This is often a cause of conflict in the workplace. Problems in communicating one's needs and thoughts or proper listening by the opposite party often leads to conflicts. Misinterpretation of communicated information can also escalate conflicts. Failure by management or the manager to address worker concerns may similarly result in conflicts.

Personality Clashes : Approximately 49% of workplace conflicts stem from differences in personalities. Variances in team members' backgrounds, outlooks, and occasionally racial biases can lead to conflicts. Divergent perspectives among colleagues may also contribute to disputes.

Workstyle Conflicts : If the employees or colleagues have different workstyles, it can lead to disagreements in the organization and pave the way for conflicts. Unresolved issues like incompatibility with a team leader, unclear expectations, or dissatisfaction with management can foster workplace conflicts.

Competing for Resources : Limited resources, such as money, materials, and equipment, can be a source of conflict when shared among employees. In settings like hospitals, where critical diagnostic or surgical equipment is shared among multiple professionals like physicians and surgeons, conflicts may arise.

In a hospital, an expensive surgical equipment was frequently utilized by various surgeons and gynecologists. However, a senior consultant consistently sought to monopolize the equipment in the operating room, depriving other consultants of the opportunity to use it. This ongoing conflict among consultants became a persistent issue, repeatedly brought to the attention of the management and Chief of Medical Services for resolution.

Ultimately, the dispute found resolution through a system that allocated the equipment to different consultants on specific days of the week, preventing them from using it on other days. Subsequently, a more enduring solution was achieved by acquiring an additional similar piece of equipment. This allowed all consultants to share the resources amicably, putting an end to the prolonged conflict.

Resistance to change : Every organization has to implement changes from time to time. Some employees may find it difficult to change and feel that the change is unwanted. This resistance to change could create a conflict between the management and the employees. People often find it difficult to move out of their comfort zones.

> In the administrative structure of an Indian state, the authorities opted to introduce digital attendance tracking for employees during their morning check-in and evening check-out. This move faced strong opposition from a faction of traditionalist employees accustomed to a more hands-off approach in government offices. The ensuing disagreement sparked a protracted conflict between the management and the workforce, necessitating an extended period for resolution.

Increased Workload : Conflicts often arise when employees feel overworked without sufficient compensation or benefits. Unrealistic expectations further contribute to conflicts between workers and management.

Leadership Conflicts : Insufficient leadership skills in managers or team leaders can fuel conflicts. At the highest levels, contention for top positions may lead to conflicts. Differing leadership styles can also cause discord among employees who do not align with their leader's ideas.

Discrimination : Workplace conflicts may arise from discrimination based on gender, race, seniority, education, age, or culture. Open-mindedness from management can mitigate these conflicts. Cultural or religious differences and employee incompatibility can also contribute to conflicts that thoughtful management can prevent.

At a government hospital where I worked, a conflict arose between two consultants within a department. Despite having identical qualifications and seniority, their inability to get along stemmed from personality clashes. Both were assigned to the outpatient department on the same day, but a discrepancy in the quality of rooms allotted to each sparked a confrontation.

This discrepancy escalated to the brink of physical violence as both consultants vied for occupancy of the superior room. Intervention became imperative, prompting the Chief of the department to step in and mediate. A resolution was achieved by scheduling the consultants on duty in the outpatient department on different days of the week, effectively diffusing the tension and putting an end to the dispute.

In this instance, the root cause of the conflict was the clash of personalities between the consultants.

Strategies for Conflict Management and Resolution

Conflicts, whether in the professional arena or personal life, are an inevitable facet of human interactions. They may manifest at the workplace, within the confines of one's home, or among members of a community. Every manager and leader is invariably tasked with the responsibility of addressing and resolving conflicts throughout their career. Acquiring this skill is paramount and necessitates dedicated training and practical experience.

Let's explore some crucial skills essential for effective conflict management.

Do not Ignore : Conflicts do not naturally dissipate. If disregarded, they have the potential to escalate into more significant issues over time. Timely resolution is imperative. Management experts advise that any recognized conflict should be addressed and neutralized within 48 hours to prevent it from smoldering and erupting into larger-scale problems. Swift action is essential to nip conflicts in the bud.

Identify and clarify the problem : Gather all relevant facts pertaining to the conflict from each party involved. The mediator should conduct separate sessions with the conflicting parties, listening patiently to their grievances. It is crucial for the mediator to maintain impartiality, ensuring a comfortable environment that does not escalate emotions, especially when dealing with sensitive information.

While engaging with the parties, the mediator should manage their emotions, avoiding anger or any hint of bias. Demonstrating empathy and active listening facilitates a successful conflict resolution. Both parties, regardless of their position within the organization, should be treated with respect to prevent any perception of discrimination during the interview. If necessary, seek additional information from third parties who witnessed the conflict, even if not directly involved. Gather as much information as possible.

Conflict resolution is a common occurrence in healthcare settings, where patients or their families may feel mistreated or inadequately cared for. Often, a senior member of management is called upon to address issues between the patient and healthcare professional. This process requires delicate handling, recognizing the heightened stress levels of both parties involved.

Bring disputants together: After identifying the source and details of the conflict and interviewing both parties, convene a meeting on neutral ground, such as the mediator's office or a conference room. It is advisable to wait until emotions have cooled down before addressing the conflict.

Encourage the disputants to express their differences and problems in the presence of the mediator, who should actively listen and remain open to suggestions.

Common Ground Rules: Establish some ground rules before commencing the meeting, emphasizing its purpose: to find a solution to the problem. Maintain a calm mood, promote honest and open discussion, and ensure that emotions are kept in check. Encourage a respectful tone and stress the confidentiality of the discussions.

Achieve a common understanding of the problem initially. Each one of the party is then asked for their suggestions for resolving the issue. Ask them to offer possible solutions to the problem. Often there may be more than one solution from each of them. The meeting should be unhurried and multiple solutions may be offered. A note of these may be made by the mediator. Continue the dialogue, asking for input from both parties.

Identify a Solution : Once the disputants have presented their solutions, work towards a mutually acceptable common ground. An open dialogue often diminishes the gravity of the problem, and parties themselves may spontaneously propose solutions. If a mutually agreeable solution is not reached, the mediator may intervene, suggesting alternatives that satisfy both parties, which may require further dialogue.

Once a solution is identified, outline the steps for implementation during the meeting, securing the agreement of both parties. Clearly define the responsibilities of each party in carrying out the agreed-upon solution.

Monitor and Follow Up : After reaching an agreement and ensuring mutual understanding between parties, the mediator must periodically check to confirm the resolution of the conflict. It is crucial to confirm the smooth functioning of the agreed-upon terms. If issues persist, an alternative, mutually acceptable solution should be identified and implemented.

Tips for Conflict Resolution:

The following summarizes suggestions for mediators and parties involved in conflict resolution:

- Establish specific guidelines for bringing parties together, maintaining proper decorum and encouraging calm, non-emotional communication.
- Avoid personal comments or criticism.
- Utilize "I" statements instead of "You" statements. For example, say *'I think that...'* or *'I feel...'* rather than *'You are wrong...'* or *'You should not...'.*
- Pose questions that elicit a positive response, such as *'Don't you feel that we should arrive at a solution quickly?'* or *'Do you think this conflict is affecting our routine?'*
- Avoid pointing fingers at each other.
- Refrain from bringing up past grievances while resolving present conflicts.
- Provide ample time for parties to express themselves in their own language; avoid rushing them.
- Demonstrate willingness to compromise and collaborate with both parties.
- Maintain a calm tone of voice during discussions and be mindful of appropriate body language. The mediator should be guarded never to lose his temper.
- Pay close attention to non-verbal cues from both parties.
- Emphasize the importance of resolving the conflict over determining right or wrong; avoid being adamant. Avoid being judgmental.
- Recognize when forgiveness and apologies are necessary.
- Stress the importance of interpersonal relationships in the organization, emphasizing that good relationships should

persist after conflict resolution.

- Encourage both parties to keep discussions confidential; the mediator should also refrain from discussing proceedings with colleagues or team members.
- Remind parties that the conflict is not personal, and the mediator holds no personal grudges. Conflict resolution is essential for the organization's smooth operation.
- Above all, exercise patience and tolerance for proper conflict resolution.

In domestic or community settings, the fundamental strategy remains the same. Conflicts may arise between partners, children, or between parents and children at home. In the community, differences of opinion among members may necessitate a third party for conflict resolution.

"An eye for an eye will only make the whole world blind"
— **Mahatma Gandhi**

8. Juggling Responsibilities – WORK-LIFE BALANCE

"If you want to change the world, go home and love your family"
– Mother Teresa

Work-life balance involves establishing a harmonious and equitable arrangement between your professional and personal spheres. It entails ensuring sufficient time and energy for work, while also dedicating time to family, friends, and leisure activities. Maintaining this equilibrium is crucial to prevent feelings of overwhelm or stress from work, promoting a fulfilling life beyond your job. Striking a balance involves managing workplace obligations alongside personal responsibilities, as neglecting family, friends, and hobbies in favor of work can negatively impact one's social and family life.

Some individuals persist in working extended hours, disregarding relationships and personal growth. They forgo leisure activities and subject themselves to excessive work-related stress, increasing the likelihood of experiencing 'burnout' over time. Research indicates that 27% of employees working long hours report feelings of depression, 34% feel anxious, and 58% experience irritability after extended work hours (Mental Health Foundation).

What Constitutes a Healthy Work-Life Balance

A healthy work-life balance entails establishing clear boundaries between one's professional commitments and personal pursuits, including time dedicated to family, friends, and leisure activities. The cornerstone of achieving this balance lies in implementing an effective time management system. The ability to adapt to varied schedules while remaining flexible is crucial, without compromising the quality of work or personal engagements. Embrace the philosophy of *working smarter, not longer.*

One has to first of all decide on one's values and what is important. We should decide what is that we strive for. What type of a parent we want to be, what type of a spouse you would like to be, what success means to you, and what your life should mean to others around you.

Identifying an unhealthy work-life balance involves recognizing several signs. Individuals who consistently work extended hours, sacrificing weekends and holidays without breaks, are on a perilous path. Ignoring personal life and relationships is a certain route to burnout. Ultimately, this neglect can strain relationships both at work and at home, posing a threat to one's overall well-being. Failing to prioritize self-care and family can result in health issues, representing the most significant harm an individual can inflict upon oneself.

Dr. Tom, (name changed), a skilled physician in a southern Indian town, was proficient in diagnosing and treating various illnesses. He interacted with patients in a pleasant manner, earning the admiration of individuals from diverse backgrounds—ranging from the less privileged to the societal elite, including administrators, politicians, and government ministers. Dr. Tom, blessed with a son and a daughter, had a dedicated homemaker wife.

His competence in patient care and exemplary bedside manner kept him occupied from 8 am to late at night. Frequently returning home after his children had gone to bed, he missed crucial moments during their formative years. Dr. Tom's commitment extended to working weekends, leaving little time for leisure.

Regrettably, this demanding professional life resulted in a disastrous family situation. His son and daughter lagged behind in studies and, as teenagers, fell into negative influences. The son struggled with drug addiction, and the daughter engaged in an affair beyond the doctor's control.

Dr. Tom belatedly recognized the consequences of his work-life imbalance. However, by then, the damage was irreversible. Experiencing a severe heart attack, he underwent bypass surgery, compelling him to reduce his hectic practice and focus on family. Despite his efforts, the fractures in family relationships proved nearly impossible to mend.

How to Enhance Work-Life Balance

Let's explore some methods to effectively balance work and personal life.

Plan Ahead: Unless one follows a pre-planned schedule, it is often difficult to balance one's work and personal life properly. One should plan a whole week of activities to be done and this can give a good balance to one's day. Clearly define your work hours and personal time and stick to them as closely as possible. Initiate and conclude work at set times, and power down work-related equipment at the end of each day.

Home Workspace Management: For those working from home, such as many in the software field today, establish a fixed 'office' time. Communicate to your family the need for private working hours, and they may respect your need for focus and concentration. Designate a quiet area or a separate room for undisturbed work, maintaining a consistent routine even in a home office setting. Avoid working on official tasks from the sofa or dining table. Do not carry work into your bedroom.

Diversify Activities: Allocate time for socializing, leisure, hobbies, fitness, and family interactions, especially with children. Incorporate a lunch break into your routine. Occasionally, socialize with co-workers for lunch or coffee, fostering connections with colleagues.

Adopting these strategies contributes to a more balanced and fulfilling life, intertwining professional responsibilities with personal well-being.

Prioritize Tasks: Effectively manage your time by focusing on the most important and urgent tasks at work and in your personal life. Setting dedicated blocks of time for various activities, as discussed earlier, is an ideal approach to accomplishing work while also allocating time for personal and other commitments.

Prioritization is crucial not only in professional but also in personal and family life. For instance, ensuring a child's annual checkup or vaccinations by taking them to the pediatrician is an essential task that cannot be overlooked. Attending a close relative's wedding is likewise a family priority. It's important to recognize that individual priorities may differ within a family, and learning to accept these differences is vital. Avoid imposing personal priorities on spouses or children.

Learn to Say No: Don't overcommit to work or personal obligations. Saying 'no' when necessary is essential. In our daily life – both work related and personal, we often take up many obligations and tasks to help others. Though it is a good habit to be helpful to others, these should not encroach on our personal or professional time thus disrupting the balance between work and life.

Take Breaks: Incorporate regular short breaks into your workday to refresh your mind and reduce stress. Adopting the *Pomodoro Technique*—working for 25 minutes followed by a 5-minute break—can alleviate stress and enhance productivity. This technique is applicable not only in the professional sphere but also in personal life. During periods of intense activity, be mindful of potential distractions. I always switch on the *Pomodoro app* on my mobile phone when I am writing a book. Taking a break every 25 minutes gives me enough time to recoup my energy to pursue writing.

Delegate: Lighten your workload by sharing tasks and responsibilities at work and home. Delegating and outsourcing are effective strategies in the office to alleviate the burden of tasks. Similarly, at home, partners can collaborate to ease the workload, and involving children in household chores not only contributes to task completion but also fosters family bonding through shared activities.

Unplug: Take a break from work emails and phone calls during your off-duty hours to truly relax and recharge. Avoid responding to office communications at home unless you're in an essential service or it's an emergency, such as in the life of a healthcare professional. Never bring work with you on vacations or picnics, as it can compromise both the quality of your leisure time and your work. Utilize modern technology, such as apps to block distracting websites, to help you disconnect. Restricting work to a single device can minimize distractions.

Enjoy life with a fulfilling hobby, whether it's painting, photography, reading, or writing. Engage in activities that bring you joy and find happiness in what you do. Embracing this approach is vital for contentment. Google has implemented a novel idea to promote creativity among its employees: dedicating 20% of their working time (one day out of five) to any project of their choosing within the employee's space. This allows employees to channel their creative energy, fostering innovative ideas and projects. This initiative is known as *Innovative Time Off*.

Exercise: Integrate regular physical activity into your routine to enhance energy levels and alleviate stress. Prioritizing one's physical well-being is as crucial as attending to one's financial health. Consistent engagement in physical activities of your choice, coupled with a healthy lifestyle, significantly contributes to enhancing both your physical and mental well-being. Schedule activities involving your entire family on weekends; this not only boosts your physical fitness but also fosters connections with your spouse and children.

Practice Mindfulness: Embrace mindfulness and meditation to remain present and reduce anxiety. The primary objective of mindfulness is to focus on the current moment. Whether at the office or a social event, refrain from dwelling on past or future concerns. Cultivate the ability to concentrate on the present, fostering relaxation and stress relief. Dedicate thirty minutes daily to practices like yoga, meditation, tai chi, as they profoundly relax both the body and mind. Learn to focus on the present moment. "*Staying in the here and now*" is the rule in mindfulness.

Plan Vacation Time: Utilize your vacation days for relaxation and rejuvenation. Resist the temptation to check work emails during your time off. Yearly vacations provide an ideal opportunity to unwind and connect with your family. Additionally, taking short breaks every three or four months contributes to recharging mental energy, allowing you to return to work with renewed vigor and enthusiasm.

Seek Support: Initiate a conversation with your employer regarding flexible work options or consider consulting with a counselor or therapist if you grapple with work-life balance. In certain situations and professions, this may be feasible. A supportive employer can play a pivotal role, especially within a positive work culture, recognizing your invaluable contribution to the organization. This may involve task streamlining and additional support to restore equilibrium in your work-life balance.

Remember, attaining a better work-life balance may necessitate trial and error to identify the strategies that suit you best. There is no universal solution for work-life balance; one must discover suitable techniques and methods, adopting a sensible lifestyle. There is no 'one-size-fits-all' solution.

Above all, refrain from pursuing perfection in all endeavors; accept reasonable outcomes as long as they are satisfactory. A healthy work-life balance effectively manages daily stress, preventing employee burnout. The organization benefits through improved employee retention,

Catherine, (name changed), served as a nurse in a large, multispecialty teaching hospital. Excelling as the top student in her nursing course, she diligently entered the workforce after earning her RN credentials, consistently putting in extra hours to make a favorable impression on her superiors and the matron.

Upon marrying an officer employed by a nationalized bank, Catherine encountered significant challenges in balancing her professional responsibilities and family life. Her husband, returning home after 5 p.m., anticipated her presence daily, but the demands of her taxing job and irregular shifts made adhering to fixed evening schedules challenging. Night shifts, in particular, left her husband disgruntled. Struggling to effectively manage both work and family, Catherine teetered on the brink of burnout. In a distressing turn, she resorted to a swift solution by ingesting a bottle of sedatives. Fortunately, timely intervention averted a catastrophe.

Following counseling sessions for both Catherine and her husband, the couple achieved a harmonious life balance. Over time, Catherine transformed into a dedicated housewife, mother, and efficient nurse, having successfully navigated the challenges that once threatened her well-being.

increased productivity, and enhanced creativity.

What Managers Should Do

- Avoid overwhelming your employees with work that they must take home.
- Provide opportunities for employees to spend time with their families, fostering camaraderie. Celebrate birthdays, wedding anniversaries, and organize occasional team events such as picnics, volunteering activities, and social clubs to enhance team relationships.
- Encourage employees to take breaks or vacations, promoting better performance upon their return. During vacations, refrain from assigning work to ensure employees can fully disconnect.
- Identify early signs of stress in employees, such as sloppiness, errors, missed deadlines, and lack of responsiveness. Provide counseling and professional help if necessary to address work-life balance issues.
- Lead by example. Hold occasional team meetings in unconventional locations, such as during a walk. Conclude virtual meetings by introducing family members, fostering a more personal connection among team members to break the monotony.
- Respect employees' working hours. Avoid scheduling meetings during lunch, late in the day, or early in the morning.
- Support working parents by providing childcare facilities for children under 5 within the organization or collaborating with nearby centers.
- Offer Employee Assistance Programs for counseling and support, addressing workplace stress, substance abuse, or relationship issues. This is available in certain organizations.

Acknowledge personal limitations and advantages. In the United States, over 60% of employees feel their work-life balance is disrupted. Harmonizing work and home life is crucial for a happy and stress-free existence.

"The key is not to prioritize what's on your schedule, but to schedule your priorities" - Stephen Covey

9. The Path to Tranquility - STRESS MANAGEMENT

"It's not stress that kills us, it's our reaction to it"
— **Hans Selye**

We are knowledge workers who engage in mental labor, relying on our minds and brains. Consequently, our brains are susceptible to fatigue and exhaustion. To enhance our productivity, it is crucial to maintain optimal relaxation and refreshment for our brains. The cognitive abilities of an individual typically decline after 7 to 8 hours of uninterrupted work. Similar to a battery, the brain requires periods of rest and recharge following prolonged activity.

Persistently working and experiencing tension can result in stress, and in severe cases, it can lead to a condition known as 'burnout.' *Burnout is a state of emotional, physical, and mental exhaustion caused by excessive and prolonged stress.* It can also be described as fatigue, frustration, or apathy resulting from prolonged stress, overwork, or intense activity. Stress is a universal experience, affecting individuals across various professions—be they doctors, nurses, scientists, high-ranking executives, government administrators, or even the ordinary homemaker.

Definition: *Stress is defined as a state of worry or mental tension caused by a difficult situation* (WHO). Hans Selye who has worked on stress has defined chronic stress as "*The response to emotional pressures suffered for a prolonged period of time which an individual perceives he or she has no control.*"

The emotions experienced during stress vary and can be described as feelings of worry, tension, fear, fatigue, depression, anxiety, frustration, or anger. Hans Selye classified stress into two types: Eustress and Distress. *Eustress* is a positive force that energizes and motivates us to instigate positive changes, while *Distress* has a negative impact.

Eustress enhances our proactivity and positivity, fostering productivity, energy, creativity, and confidence. Examples include significant life events like purchasing a new home, getting married, having a child, engaging in physical exercise, public speaking, starting a new job, or traveling. These experiences lead to constructive and beneficial outcomes.

Conversely, distress carries negative implications and denotes an unpleasant state. Events such as the death of a loved one, divorce, job loss, conflicts with colleagues, financial problems, illness, or accidents fall under distress. Unlike eustress, distress results in destructive consequences and adverse health effects.

Symptoms of Stress.

Stress can induce physical, mental, behavioral, or emotional manifestations.

Physical Symptoms : In cases of chronic stress, physical symptoms predominantly impact the body, leading to various health issues. Immunity reduction is a common consequence, making individuals more susceptible to frequent illnesses. Common stress-related symptoms include muscle pain, especially in the neck, shoulders, and lower back. Additionally, stressed individuals may experience an increased incidence of arthritis.

Chronic stress increases the risk of heart disease, potentially culminating in a heart attack. High blood pressure, prevalent in the modern age, is often linked to stress. Stress can also act as a catalyst for strokes. Frequent headaches and migraines are commonly associated with stress.

Furthermore, stress can contribute to the development of stomach ulcers and medical conditions such as Gastroesophageal Reflux Disease (GERD) and Irritable Bowel Syndrome (IBS). Reproductive systems may be affected, leading to issues such as low fertility, erectile problems in males, and painful menstruation in females.

Dermatological conditions, including acne and neurodermatitis, are often stress-related. Psoriasis, a skin disease, tends to flare up during periods of heightened stress.

Acute stress can manifest as palpitations, breathlessness, or dizziness. In some instances, stressed individuals may experience acute panic attacks.

Mental Symptoms : Numerous mental symptoms accompany stress. Both depression and anxiety can stem from stress. Outbursts of anger and losing one's temper are common in cases of chronic stress. The individual struggles to concentrate and becomes overly concerned about minor matters. Jumpiness and persistent fatigue often accompany chronic stress, leading to the development of "*Tired All The Time*" (TATT) syndrome.

Behavioral symptoms : Behavioral manifestations encompass frequent procrastination, smoking, alcohol, and drug abuse, nail-biting, restlessness, irritability, anger, impulsiveness, and forgetfulness. Insomnia frequently manifests as a symptom of chronic stress. Those close to the individual readily notice changes in mood and personality.

Emotional Symptoms : Emotional symptoms of stress involve heightened irritability, mood swings, an inability to relax the mind, low self-esteem, feelings of worthlessness, depression, social avoidance, relationship breakdowns, a sense of being overwhelmed, frequent crying, trouble concentrating, and decision-making difficulties.

Workplace Stress

What can workplace stress lead to. It can result in various issues for individuals. Some of these concerns are outlined below:

- Stressed individuals may encounter challenges at work, such as difficulties in relationships, task delays, and ineffective communication.
- It can adversely affect relationships with colleagues.
- Overall working environment issues may contribute to team conflicts, a lack of cooperation, and coordination problems.
- Employees' decision-making abilities and concentration can suffer, leading to diminished productivity.
- In certain settings, like factories or other essential organizations, stress might contribute to accidents.
- Increased likelihood of errors by stressed employees.
- Customer complaints may rise if employee performance declines due to stress.
- In critical organizations, such as healthcare institutions, staff stress can have catastrophic consequences.
- Stress may also lead to higher employee absenteeism due to health issues.

Some workplace stressors include the following factors:

- Insecurity about job stability.
- Interpersonal conflicts among colleagues or between employees and management.
- Excessive workload within tight timeframes.
- Insufficient compensation coupled with elevated performance expectations.
- Prolonged working hours, particularly evident in professions

like healthcare, with demanding deadlines and long working hours for doctors and nurses.

- Uncomfortable physical working conditions such as inadequate ventilation, excessive heat, or subpar facilities.
- Discrepancies between employee expectations and company policies.
- Managing interactions with dissatisfied and impolite customers is an important stressor for many employees.

Strategies for Managing and Avoiding Stress

Managing stress is crucial for a happy and successful life, promoting overall well-being. Recognizing stressors in our lives is vital for maintaining balance and a stress-free existence. According to the American Psychological Association, 67% of Americans reported increased stress post-Covid. Common stressors include work, health, finances, family, and relationships. Individuals vary in their ability to withstand pressure, necessitating tailored stress management strategies.

> Dr. Peter, (name changed) a resident in a specific hospital department, was one of four sons in a financially challenged farming family. Recently, he faced personal challenges at home, leading to chronic stress that hindered his focus on hospital work. Consequently, he incurred the Chief of the department's displeasure, frequently submitting project work late and neglecting preparation for weekly case presentations. Interactions with fellow residents also posed challenges.
>
> Clearly, stress significantly affected Dr. Peter. The Chief Coordinator of Residents and I collaborated to address this issue. Multiple counseling sessions were scheduled to address his genuine problems, which were impeding his departmental performance. After six months of intensive counseling and discussions, we successfully helped him overcome stress, transforming his mindset towards departmental work.
>
> By breaking free from stress-induced non-performance, Dr. Peter completed his residency program successfully.

Key Stress Management Strategies:

1. <u>Identify Stress Sources:</u> We have already discussed the causes of stress and the stressors. The stressors differ among different individuals according to their psychological makeup and hence each individual should endeavor to identify the root cause of his stress. Ideally, these should be written down. Also

what the stressor caused in your behaviour or work should be noted. What really relieved the stress may be noted. Once this has been done over a period of time, Consistent self-reflection allows insight into one's stress triggers and potential coping mechanisms, facilitating a proactive approach to stress management.

2. <u>Avoid Unhealthy Coping:</u> Resist unhealthy practices like smoking, excessive alcohol consumption, drug use, junk food indulgence, prolonged sleep, social isolation, and expressing stress through anger. Opt for healthier alternatives to effectively cope with stress.

3. <u>Avoid Stressors:</u> Recognize predictable stressors and adopt proactive measures. One may feel stressed while driving to work in the morning due to the heavy traffic congestion. An ideal solution would be to take a different route to the office where the traffic would be less. Alternatively, one could commute to work using the metro rail or other modes of public transport which is less stressful. If the To-do-list for the day is too crowded, you could pare it down a little and postpone a couple of tasks for the next day. If certain topics like politics or religion gets you worked up, you could avoid such discussions. There are certain people who have an uncanny knack of causing you stress – steer clear of them.

4. <u>Change the situation:</u> When avoidance is impractical, consider altering the circumstances. If possible, you could walk away from a stressful situation, or you could openly express your feelings if a person is constantly giving you stress. Instead of bottling up one's feelings, they could be discussed freely, openly and without animosity or anger. Seeking compromise can be effective. Occasionally, it is better to tackle the situation and 'take the bull by the horns' instead of running away from the situation. Be assertive in situations

where you have to be so. Learn to balance your life and your work.

5. <u>Avoid being a perfectionist:</u> Perfectionism often leads to stress for many individuals, but this isn't necessary in every situation. Recognize that there are instances where perfection is not required. Set reasonably attainable standards and be gentle with yourself. Take a moment to evaluate whether the situation is genuinely worth stressing over; the answer might surprise you.

6. <u>Accept things you can't change</u>: Embrace the acceptance of things beyond your control. Recall the Serenity prayer:

> *God Grant me the Serenity*
> *To accept the things I cannot change,*
> *The courage to change the things I can,*
> *And the wisdom to know the difference.*

Worrying about uncontrollable factors such as climate, weather, national financial crises, or recession is futile. Death and illness are inevitable aspects of life, causing initial stress that should be acknowledged and then overcome. While you can modify your behavior and reactions to circumstances, you cannot change others. Accept this fact, harmonize with those around you, and forgive mistakes. Recognize that the world is imperfect, and instead of dwelling on errors, learn to forgive, allowing personal growth. Count your blessings, share your feelings with a confidant. *Stress shared is stress halved.*

1. <u>Exercise</u> Incorporate exercise into your routine. Physical activity is an effective stress reliever, triggering the release of endorphins, the 'feel-good' hormone. Even a brief ten or fifteen-minute workout or walk can significantly alleviate

stress. Engage in activities like dancing to music, listening to soothing music, strolling in the park, or opting for using the stairs over elevators.

2. <u>Connect with friends:</u> Sharing your thoughts with someone can alleviate stress. Take breaks with friends over coffee, enjoy dinner dates, or reconnect with old acquaintances. Go to the church, temple or mosque and sit quietly for some time in reflection. Connecting with family and friends, joining social clubs, volunteering to help others, or spending time with elderly parents can be therapeutic. Spend some time with children. A hug from a loved one or hugging a pet is said to relieve acute stress.

3. <u>Leisure time Activities:</u> Dedicate time to activities you enjoy. whether it's going to the beach, playing the piano, drawing, painting, carpentry, or watching a humorous movie. Learning to laugh at yourself is a valuable coping mechanism. Destress yourself watching a '*Tom and Jerry*' cartoon.

> During my residency in the Department of Medicine many years ago, I faced a challenging phase in my career. Working continuously for 36 hours without a break had taken a toll, pushing me to the brink of burnout. My close friend, who shared the residency with me, was also grappling with similar stress. In search of a solution, we decided to explore meditation.
>
> We enrolled in a session where a Guru taught Transcendental Meditation, as advocated by Maharishi Mahesh Yogi. Under the Guru's guidance, we underwent training, committing to practicing 20 minutes of meditation both in the morning and evening. Surprisingly, within a few days of adopting this routine, I started experiencing an unusual inner calm, allowing me to navigate daily life stress more effectively. This positive change encouraged me to persist with the meditation practice.
>
> Even today, when I find myself overwhelmed, I prioritize a 15 to 20-minute meditation session. This practice helps me reconnect with inner peace, restoring my calm and recharging my emotional batteries.

4. <u>Practice relaxation methods.</u> Incorporate Yoga, Meditation, Tai-chi, and Deep Breathing into your routine to relax and destress. Aroma therapy, using essential oils like sandalwood and lavender, can be beneficial. Place a scented candle or fresh fragrant flowers in your space for stress relief. Listening to

soothing meditation music at a low volume while reclining aids relaxation. Meditation fosters mindfulness, allowing you to savor the present moment and ease both body and soul.

11. <u>Efficient Time Management:</u> Employing effective time management principles and being properly organized significantly reduces stress in the workplace. A meticulously planned day is instrumental in alleviating stress.

12. <u>Simplify your Life:</u> Establish priorities for crucial aspects of life and minimize unnecessary, unproductive tasks. Learn to say *"No"* and decline additional responsibilities when overwhelmed, and delegate or outsource tasks when feasible. Avoid taking on more than you can handle.

13. <u>Raise a pet:</u> Many find pets to be excellent stress relievers. Raising a pet and dedicating daily time to them can be a therapeutic way to destress and enhance mood.

14. <u>Adopt a Healthy Lifestyle:</u> Maintaining proper nutrition, regular exercise, and cultivating good habits are vital for mental and physical well-being, significantly reducing stress. A balanced diet, including lean protein, complex carbohydrates, fruits, and vegetables, contributes to a healthy lifestyle. Opt for healthy snacks, ensure 7-8 hours of quality sleep, and abstain from alcohol, smoking, and drugs.

15. <u>Explore Religion and Spirituality:</u> For many, engaging in religious and spiritual practices aids in coping with daily stressors. Visiting places of worship, such as churches, temples, or mosques, can provide solace. Establishing a morning prayer routine and seeking guidance from religious

figures like priests or sadhus can be calming. Listening to religious discourses and participating in group activities like bhajans and choirs also contribute to stress relief.

"A crust eaten in peace is better than a banquet partaken in anxiety."
— Aesop

RESOURCES

Reference Books

1. Master Your Time. Master Your Life : Brian Tracy. Penguin Random House. 2017.

2. The Essential Manager's Handbook: Editor. Chauney Dunford Penguin Random House. 2022.

3. How to Win Friends and Influence People: Dale Carnegie. Pocket books 1998.

4. How Management Works. Philippa Anderson. Penguin Random House 2020.

5. How to Stop Worrying & Start Living : Dale Carnegie. (Reprint) True Sign Publishing house 2021.

6. 100 Ways to Motivate Others. 3rd Ed. Steve Chandler, Scott Richardson. Career Press. 2012.

7. Never Get Angry Again : David J Lieberman. St. Martin Press. New York. 2017.

8. Anger Management for Everyone : Raymond Chip Tafrale, Howard Kassinove 2nd Ed. Impact Publishers. Oakland CA. 2019.

9. The Art of Public Speaking. Dale Carnegie. (Reprint). Clydesdale Press. 2018.

Articles, Blogs, Podcasts.

<u>Time Management</u>

1. Time Management Strategies for Artists: Balancing Creativity, Productivity and Life. ACT International. 2023.

https://www.actinternational.org/articles/time-management-strategies-for-

artists?campaignid=19995375267&adgroupid=157337216121&adid=674634468378
U5pHUcebt3knuxY3sHB5nnAvXSSihoCGdQQAvD_BwE

1. **18** Effective Time Management Strategies : Sean Cope 2021.

https://www.upwork.com/resources/time-management-strategies

1. Introducing the Eisenhower Matrix :

Source: https://luxafor.com/the-eisenhower-matrix/

1. Pomodoro Technique : Wikipedia 2023.

Pomodoro Technique - Wikipedia[1]

1. What is Time Management. **6** Strategies to Better Manage your Time. : Coursera 2023.

https://www.coursera.org/articles/time-management

1. Time Management. **10** Strategies for Better Time Management. Sue W. Chapman, Michael Rupured, Roxie Price, Dana Carnie, Rachael Clews. University of Georgia Extension. 2022.

https://extension.uga.edu/publications/
detail.html?number=C1042&title=time-management-10-strategies-for-
better-time-management

1. Time Management Skills, Techniques and Strategies – The Ultimate List. : My Hours 2022.

https://myhours.com/articles/time-management-skills-techniques-
strategies-list

1. **8** Time Management Tips for Students. Lian Parsons. Harvard School of

---

1.   https://en.wikipedia.org/wiki/Pomodoro_Technique

Continuing Education. 2022.

https://summer.harvard.edu/blog/8-time-management-tips-for-students/

1. **8** Essential Time Management Strategies. :Missy Day. Liquid Planner -the blog for passionate planners.

https://www.liquidplanner.com/blog/8-essential-time-management-strategies/

1. What is Time Management. : Mind Tools Content Team. 2023.

https://www.mindtools.com/arb6j5a/what-is-time-management

1. **22** Effective Time Management Strategies for Work : Sandeep Kashyap. Proof Hub. 2023.

https://www.proofhub.com/articles/time-management-strategies

1. Top 16 Time Management Skills to Help you Become a Success : Simplilearn. 2023.

https://www.simplilearn.com/time-management-skills-article

Communication Skills.

1. How Great Leaders Communicate : Carmine Gallo. Harvard Business Review. 2022.

https://hbr.org/2022/11/how-great-leaders-communicate

1. 6 Communication Skills Every Manager should Master : David Grossman. 2023.

https://www.yourthoughtpartner.com/blog/communication-skills-for-managers

1. 10 Tips for Effective Communication in the Workplace : Christana Jolaoso in Forbes Advisor 2023.

https://www.forbes.com/advisor/business/effective-communication-workplace/

1. Management Communication. 18 Ways Managers can Improve it. : Editorial Team. Indeed Career Development. 2023.

https://www.indeed.com/career-advice/career-development/management-of-communication

1. 15 Tips for Effective Communication in Leadership.: Leading effectively staff. Center for Creative Leadership. 2023.

https://www.ccl.org/articles/leading-effectively-articles/communication-1-idea-3-facts-5-tips/

1. 8 Ways you Can Improve Your Communication Skills. : Mary Sharp Emerson. Harvard Division of Continuing Education. 2021.

https://professional.dce.harvard.edu/blog/8-ways-you-can-improve-your-communication-skills/

1. Communication Skills for Managers : Business Victoria (Blog) 2023.

https://business.vic.gov.au/business-information/staff-and-hr/staff-management/communication-skills-in-the-workplace-for-managers

1. Effective Communication : HelpGuide.org. Robinson L, Segal J, Smith M. 2023.

https://www.helpguide.org/articles/relationships-communication/effective-communication.htm

1. 18 Effective Strategies to Improve Your Communication Skills :Nicolas Gattig. Better Up. 2023.

https://www.betterup.com/blog/effective-strategies-to-improve-your-communication-skills

1. 10 Communication Skills for your Life and Career Success : Genevieve Northup. Indeed. Career guide 2023.

https://www.indeed.com/career-advice/resumes-cover-letters/communication-skills

1. A Breakdown of 10 Essential Communication Skill Examples for the Workplace : Alec Bailon. edapp.

https://www.edapp.com/blog/communication-skills-examples/

1. 66 Communications Skills Examples (A to Z List) : Chris Drew. HelpfulProfessor.com.

https://helpfulprofessor.com/communication-skills-examples/

Doctor (Nurse) – Patient Communication

1. Doctor Patient Communication : A Review. Fong Ha J, Longnecker N. Ochsner J.[2] 2010 Spring; 10(1): 38–43

https://www.ncbi.nlm.nih.gov/pmc/articles/PMC3096184/

1. Doctor-Patient Communication : Guidelines and Best Practices. Paget SA, Mazie B. (Adapted from a presentation at the SLE Workshop and Myositis support group- Hospital for Special Surgery) 2019.

https://www.hss.edu/conditions_doctor-patient-communication.asp

1. Patient Relations : The Importance of Doctor Patient Communication. Lecturio Medical Student blog. : Villanueva B. 2023.

---

2. https://www.ncbi.nlm.nih.gov/pmc/articles/PMC3096184/

https://www.lecturio.com/blog/medical/patient-relations-the-importance-of-doctor-patient-communication/

1. Do's and Don'ts for Effective Doctor-Patient Communication.: Moyer K. Rendia. 2023.

https://rendia.com/resources/insights/dos-donts-effective-doctor-patient-communication/

1. How to Improve Your Doctor-Patient Communication : Goldman A. Nexhealth. 2023.

https://www.nexhealth.com/resources/how-to-improve-your-doctor-patient-communication

Breaking Bad News

1. Breaking Bad News. Gregg. K. Vandekieft. Amer. Fam. Physician. 2001;64(12):1975-1979.

https://www.aafp.org/pubs/afp/issues/2001/1215/p1975.html

1. Breaking Bad News. A Guide for Effective and Empathetic Communication. Rosenzweig. MQ. Nurse Pract. 2012 Feb 12;37(2):1-4.

https://www.ncbi.nlm.nih.gov/pmc/articles/PMC5578619/

1. Breaking Bad News. Tony Back. UW Medicine 2018.

https://depts.washington.edu/bhdept/ethics-medicine/bioethics-topics/detail/55

1. SPIKES – A SixStep Protocol for Delivering Bad News: Application to the Patient with Cancer : Baile WF, Buckman R, Lenzi R, Glober G, Beale EA, Kudelka AP (2000) Oncologist 5:302-311

https://www.cetl.org.uk/learning/feedback_opportunities/data/downloads/breaking_bad_news.pdf

1. Breaking Bad News to Patients and Relatives : Chris Nickson. Life in the Fast Lane 2022.

https://litfl.com/breaking-bad-news-to-patients-and-relatives/

1. 9 Tips for Delivering Bad News. Braga-Melle R, Day SH, Schwab IR. American Academy of Ophthalmology. 2023.

https://www.aao.org/eyenet/young-ophthalmologist/
tips-delivering-bad-news

1. Beyond breaking bad news: how to help patients that suffer. Rabow MW, McPhee SJ. West J Med 1999;171:261.

https://www.cetl.org.uk/learning/feedback_opportunities/data/
downloads/breaking_bad_news.pdf

1. Bereavement and How to Help Families when Patients Die. Fallat ME. Mayo Clinic 2021.

https://www.mayoclinic.org/medical-professionals/trauma/news/
bereavement-and-how-to-help-families-when-patients-die/mac-
20522945

Interpersonal Skills

1. Interpersonal Skills. Skillsyouneed.

https://www.skillsyouneed.com/interpersonal-skills.html

1. What are Interpersonal Skills ? Definition with examples. Roma Konczak. Zety. 2023.

https://zety.com/blog/interpersonal-skills

1. Top 10 Interpersonal Skills and Why they matter to Employers : Jill Wells. Wellsgray Recruitment. 2020.

https://www.wellsgray.com.au/blog/top-10-interpersonal-skills-why-they-matter-to-employers

1. Nine Tips for Improving Your Interpersonal Skills : Kelly

https://www.kellyservices.ca/ca/careers/career-resource-centre/managing-your-career/nine-tips-for-improving-your-interpersonal-skills/

1. Boost your Interpersonal Skills : Mindtools Content Team. Mindtools. 2023.

https://www.mindtools.com/anmomb0/boost-your-interpersonal-skills

1. 10 Important Interpersonal Skills [with Examples] : Abby McCain. Zippia 2023.

https://www.zippia.com/advice/interpersonal-skills/
Clinical Handover

1. Nursing Clinical Handover. Stacey Richards. The Royal Children's Hospital Melbourne. 2023.

https://www.rch.org.au/rchcpg/hospital_clinical_guideline_index/Nursing_clinical_handover/

1. Communication at Clinical Handover. Australian Commission on Safety and Quality in Health Care. 2023.

https://www.safetyandquality.gov.au/standards/nsqhs-standards/communicating-safety-standard/communication-clinical-handover

1. Clinical Handover Guide : Government of Western Australia Department of Health. 2017.

https://www.health.wa.gov.au/~/media/Files/Corporate/general-documents/Quality/PDF/Clinical-Handover-Guideline.pdf

1. Handing Over Care : Victoria Department of Health. Australia. 2015.

https://www.health.vic.gov.au/patient-care/handing-over-care

1. Communication During Patient Handovers : The Joint Commission International. World Health Organization. Vol. 1. Solution 3. May 2007.

https://cdn.who.int/media/docs/default-source/patient-safety/patient-safety-solutions/ps-solution3-communication-during-patient-handovers.pdf

1. Teaching Clinical Handover with ISBAR. Burgess, A., van Diggele, C., Roberts, C. *et al.* Teaching clinical handover with ISBAR. *BMC Med Educ* **20** (Suppl 2), 459 (2020).

https://bmcmededuc.biomedcentral.com/articles/10.1186/s12909-020-02285-0

1. Safety of handover: a global online survey of clinical practitioners and leaders regarding patient safety during transitions of care. Hamblin Brown DJ, Craggs J et al. *Preprints* **2022**, 2022050202. https://doi.org/10.20944/preprints202205.0202.v2

file:///C:/Users/DELL/Downloads/preprints202205.0202.v2.pdf

Conflict Management

1. The Top 5 Conflict Resolution Strategies for the Workplace : Sonya Krakoff. Champlain College Online. 2023.

https://online.champlain.edu/blog/top-conflict-resolution-strategies

1. Conflict Resolution : Mind Tools Content Team . MindTools. 2023.

https://www.mindtools.com/ahcpfn4/conflict-resolution

1. Conflict Management : Definition, Strategies and Styles : Coursera. 2023.

https://www.coursera.org/articles/conflict-management

1. 7 Tips on How to Manage and Resolve Conflict in the Workplace: Allen Cranston. HR Cloud 2021.

https://www.hrcloud.com/blog/7-tips-on-how-to-manage-and-resolve-conflict-in-the-workplace

1. 14 Conflict Resolution Strategies for the Workplace. : Christina R. Wilson, Anna K Schaffner Positive Workplace. 2022.

https://positivepsychology.com/conflict-resolution-in-the-workplace/

1. 27 Conflict Resolution Skills to Use With Your Team and Your Customers. Swetha Amaresan. Hubspot. 2023.

https://blog.hubspot.com/service/conflict-resolution-skills

1. Kauth, K. (2020, January). *Cost of workplace conflict*. Mediate.com. Retrieved November 27, 2021, from

https://mediate.com/cost-of-workplace-conflict/
Work-Life Balance

1. Ten Tips for Better Work-Life Balance : Stuart Jeffries. The Guardian – Life and Style. 2014.

file:///C:/BOOK-%20MGMT/MGMT-PPTS/
PPT%20ON%20SKILL%20TRAINING/
STRESS%20MGMT%20IMAGES/
Ten%20tips%20for%20a%20better%20work-life%20balance%20_%20Life%20and%20

1. How to have a Good Work-Life Balance. : Allaya Cooks-Campbell. Betterup. 2023.

https://www.betterup.com/blog/how-to-have-good-work-life-balance

1. 10 Work-Life Balance Tips. Your Complete Guide for 2023. Radhika Basuthakur. Upwork. 2023.

https://www.upwork.com/resources/work-life-balance-tips

1. 25 Best ways to achieve Work-Life Balance and its Benefits : Angshuman and Thadoi. Vantage Circle. 2023.

https://blog.vantagecircle.com/work-life-balance/

1. Work-Life Balance : Mental Health Foundation. 2021.

https://www.mentalhealth.org.uk/explore-mental-health/a-z-topics/work-life-balance

1. 20 Essential Tips for Ultimate Work-Life Balance : Electra Michaelidou. CareerAddict 2019.

https://www.careeraddict.com/work-life-balance-tips

1. 10 Easy Ways to Practice Mindfulness at Work : Joanna Zambas. CareerAddict. 2018.

10 Easy Ways to Practice Mindfulness at Work (careeraddict.com)[3]
Stress Management

1. Ways to Manage Stress : Lauren Ragland. WebMD 2023.

https://www.webmd.com/balance/stress-management/stress-management

1. Manage Stress and Regain Control with 20 Tips to Better Living.: Maggie Wooll. Betterup 2022.

https://www.betterup.com/blog/stress-management-techniques

1. Stress Management. How to Reduce and Relieve Stress : Lawrence Robinson, Melinda Smith. Helpguide.org. 2023.

https://www.helpguide.org/articles/stress/stress-management.htm

---

3. https://www.careeraddict.com/mindfulness-work

1. 5 Tips to Manage Stress : Brian Hessler. Mayo Clinic Health System. 2023.

https://www.mayoclinichealthsystem.org/hometown-health/
speaking-of-health/5-tips-to-manage-stress

1. How to Manage Stress. 13 Ways to Feel Better Fast : Emily Guarnotta, India B Gomez. GoodRx Health. 2023.

https://www.goodrx.com/conditions/stress/stress-management-tips-
techniques

1. 11 Healthy ways to handle Life's Stressors : Beverly Thorn. American Psychological Association. 2022.

https://www.apa.org/topics/stress/tips

1. Stress Management Skills : Madhuri Thakur. EDUCBA 2023.

https://www.educba.com/stress-management-skills/

1. Stress Management : Wikipedia. 2023.

https://en.wikipedia.org/wiki/Stress_management

1. Stress Management : Romito K, Sproule D, Husney A, Locke S.- Healthwise Staff. Healthlink BC 2021.

https://www.healthlinkbc.ca/health-topics/stress-management

1. How to Manage and Reduce Stress : Mental Health Foundation. 2023.

https://www.mentalhealth.org.uk/explore-mental-health/publications/
how-manage-and-reduce-stress

1. Mindfulness Meditation: A Research Proven Way to Reduce Stress: David J Creswell, Bassam Khoury. American Psychological Association. 2019.

<u>Mindfulness meditation: A research-proven way to reduce stress (apa.org)</u>[4]

4. https://www.apa.org/topics/mindfulness/meditation

A Humble Request to the Reader

Thank you for buying and reading this book. May I request your indulgence for one more favor.

I hope you enjoyed reading this book and derived benefit from the assorted topics discussed.

Kindly give your sincere and valuable review of this book. Your rating and candid review will be a great inspiration and encouragement to me.

I would also request you to check my other books – *Tell Me a Story, Grandpa* and *Grandpa Tell Me More Stories* which are a compilation of short stories with morals, written with children in mind.

Also, the book of '*In Search of a Bridegroom*' is an interesting Autobiographical Fiction which will be of great interest to the reader.

Two books on the Health Problems faced by the Elderly are available under the names, "*How to face the Health Challenges While getting Old*" and "*Old Age Health – Challenges and Solutions*" These deal with the Health Challenges in old age, their Early Recognition, Prevention and Treatment.

My recent medical book named "*Understanding the Electrocardiogram*" is a book written for the benefit of the Medical fraternity. It is a book for doctors, residents, and nurses.

The book "*Demystifying Hinduism*" is a book describing the Basics of Hinduism in a simple manner and is Book 1 of the series '*Understanding Hinduism*'. The second book "*The Avadhoota*" in the series describes the journey of a monk in search of truth from Nature. The book "*Daily Musings*" is a collection of sixty inspirational messages for daily living.

Thank you for your Co-operation.

APPENDIX

MORE BOOKS BY THE AUTHOR

How to Face the Challenges while Growing Old
Old Age Health Challenges and Solutions
(Problems of Old Age Series)

This is a series of two books dealing with the Health Problems faced by the Elderly. Most of the Systems of the human body and their problems are discussed in the books. Recognition of the symptoms of the various diseases of old age and their prevention are discussed. The available modalities of treatment are mentioned in brief. This is a book for the public and not for the medical profession. It makes the average person aware of what he will face when he becomes older.

Tell Me a Story, Grandpa
Grandpa, Tell me More Stories
(Children's Short Stories Series)

This a series of books of Short Stories for children. The books abound in short stories imparting morals and values which will fascinate and entertain children. Ideal for children in the school going age. The books provide excellent bed time stories for children. Each book has 40 such stories that will keep children entertained during the holidays. The books are ideal to be gifted to children on birthdays and other festivals. The books are recommended to be added to the school libraries.

Understanding the Electrocardiogram
(For the Doctor's Pocket)

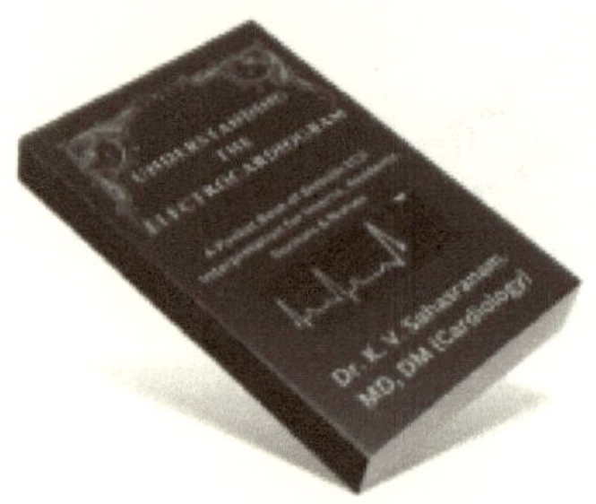

A simple Pocket Book of interpreting the Electrocardiogram which can be carried during Ward Rounds and in the ICU. Interpretation of ECG is explained in simple language with more than 150 illustrations and ECG tracings.

The book is in 3 parts - *12 Lead ECG Interpretations, Arrhythmias-Disorders of Impulse Generation - Arrhythmias - Disorders of Impulse Conduction.*

Immensely Useful for Doctors, General & Family Practitioners, Medical Students, Interns, Residents, Nurses, and Paramedics. It makes the methodical interpretation of ECGs a child's play.

Demystifying Hinduism
(Understanding Hinduism – Book 1)

Hinduism, which is truly named "*Sanatana Dharma*" is undergoing a great revival in the Modern World. The Hindu Diaspora which is spread all over the world find it difficult to understand and learn the basics of Hinduism. The new generation of Hindu youth also need to get to know the Foundation of Hinduism.

This book describes the Basic Facts about Hinduism in a simple language for easy understanding. The book which is in a Question & Answer format, discusses, the origin of Religion, the Hindu Scriptures, the Idol worship and its symbolism, Rituals and Temple Worship, Yoga, Dharma, Meditation and Hindu Festivals. The Varna Ashrama system, Death & Reincarnation, and the Concept of Time in Hinduism are elaborately, but clearly described.

The Avadhoota – Whispers of Wisdom
Daily Musings – Nourishment for your Soul
(Understanding Hinduism Book 2)

The book **"The Avadhoota"** presents a fictionalized rendition of the Yadu-Avadhoota Samvadam found in the Srimad Bhagavatham. Within its pages, the author eloquently portrays the Twenty-four Gurus as originally described by the Avadhoota. The narrative follows the journey of the Brahmachari sage Datta, who embarks on a nationwide expedition to glean experiential insights into the various teachings of Hindu philosophy.

To enhance the textual variety, the author presents the chapter summaries in the form of verses injecting a rhythmic cadence that complements the overall content.

The book **"Daily Musings"** is a garland of 60 inspirational and motivational passages for everyday living.

In Search of a Bridegroom
(An Autobiographical Fiction)

An interesting Autobiographical Fiction, where the author takes the reader through the journey where he was in search of a bridegroom for his daughter. Interesting anecdotes and embarrassing circumstances are described by the author in an amusing manner and finally, he succeeds in finding an appropriate groom for his daughter. The book is based on true facts and combines moments of suspense and hilarious incidents.

ACKNOWLEDGEMENTS

I would like to express my sincere gratitude to the Chairman and Managing Director of Baby Memorial Hospital, Dr. K. G. Alexander. As the Chief of Medical Services and Senior Consultant in Cardiology, his guidance and support have been invaluable in navigating complex situations.

Special thanks go to Ms. Gracy Mathai, the CEO of Baby Memorial Hospital, whose unwavering support, and mentorship have been crucial during my tenure. Her expertise in management has been instrumental in honing my skills for leading a large group of doctors and residents.

I am also thankful to Mr. Saji Mathew, the COO of the hospital, for his multifaceted role in managing the IT and HR departments. His inspiration and guidance in leadership and management principles have greatly contributed to my role as the Chief of Medical Services.

I extend my gratitude to the members of the Hospital Management Committee for their consistent support. There was always something to learn from each of them. The staff in the Quality and H.R. departments too have been very helpful in assisting me in my efforts.

Throughout my management tenure, I gleaned insights not only from top leaders but also from my fellow doctors, nurses, managers, residents, and other staff across various departments. Their collective contributions played a pivotal role in the successful completion of my term as the Medical Director.

The inspiration for this book was drawn from a variety of sources such as library books, podcasts, YouTube videos, TED talks, and blogs. I sincerely thank the authors of these mediums for their valuable contributions.

A special mention goes to my family, whose unwavering support was indispensable during the challenging process of authoring this book. Their encouragement was a constant source of strength and motivation, and I acknowledge their pivotal role in this endeavor. My daughter, Sandya, has been of immense help in formatting and assisting with the technological aspects of my endeavor.

My thanks to Lolitha of Revandesigns for the excellent book cover.

I also want to extend my thanks to Mr. Som Bathla, my mentor on this authorial journey, and the supportive members of the Author-Helping-Author (AHA) community. Their constructive suggestions at various stages of writing and publishing have been invaluable.

COPYRIGHT

<u>DISCLAIMER</u>

The information presented in the book, including facts and statistics, is sourced from reliable and authentic references. The book conveys the author's personal suggestions and opinions. Notably, the author has made a conscientious effort to safeguard the identities of individuals involved in real incidents from his career. These incidents are cited solely for illustrative purposes and not with the intent to disparage any individual or institution.

ABOUT THE AUTHOR

Dr. K. V. Sahasranam (Sahasranam Kalpathy) is the author of nine books previously on various subject like Short stories for children, an Autobiographical fiction, a book on ECG and two books on Health Problems in Old age. He has been practicing as a Senior Consultant Cardiologist in a multispecialty hospital in India and was the Chief of Medical Services there.

His books of Short Stories with morals, for children are named 'Tell Me A Story, Grandpa' and 'Grandpa, Tell Me More Stories.' His third book 'In Search of a Bridegroom' is an Autobiographical fiction based on his first-hand experiences. He has authored two books in a series dealing with the Health Problems of Elderly persons namely 'How to face the Health Challenges While Growing Old' and 'Old Age Health – Challenges and Solutions.' His book on 'Understanding the Electrocardiogram' is a handbook for doctors, medical residents, and nurses. His recent book is 'Demystifying Hinduism' which describes the Basics of Hinduism in a Q & A format. His second book, recently published, is 'The Avadhoota – Whispers of Wisdom'. It is a fictionalized rendition of the Yadu-Avadhoota Samvadam found in the Srimad Bhagavatham describing the Avadhoota and his twenty-four Gurus from Nature. The book "*Daily Musings*" is a collection of sixty inspirational messages for daily living.

He is a retired Cardiologist settled in the U.S.

About the Author

Sahasranam Kalpathy (Dr. K. V. Sahasranam) is the author of nine books previously on various subjects like Short stories for children, an Autobiographical fiction, a book on 'Understanding the Electrocardiogram' and two books on 'Health Problems in Old Age'. His first book on 'Understanding Hinduism series' is named "Demystifying Hinduism". His second book "The Avadhoota" describes another interesting aspect of Hinduism. In the book "Daily Musings" he has given inspirational messages for daily living derived from the scriptures and Hindu Mythology.

In this book he has described the skills needed to be successful in life from the point of view of a Medical Director.

He is a Cardiologist settled in the U.S.

www.ingramcontent.com/pod-product-compliance
Lightning Source LLC
Chambersburg PA
CBHW030334160726
47987CB00021B/497